JOHNNY
FOOTBALL

JOHNNY
FOOTBALL

Johnny Manziel's Wild Ride
from Obscurity to Legend
at Texas A&M

Mike Shropshire

MVP
BOOKS

First published in 2014 by MVP Books, an imprint of Quarto Publishing Group USA Inc.,
400 First Avenue North, Suite 400, Minneapolis, MN 55401 USA

MVP Books titles are also available at discounts in bulk quantity for industrial or
sales-promotional use. For details write to Special Sales Manager at Quarto Publishing
Group USA Inc., 400 First Avenue North, Suite 400, Minneapolis, MN 55401 USA.

To find out more about our books, visit us online at www.mvpbooks.com.

ISBN-13: 978-0-7603-4626-6

Library of Congress Control Number: 2014934760

Acquisitions Editor: Josh Leventhal
Project Manager: Madeleine Vasaly
Design Manager: James Kegley

On the front cover: Johnny Manziel looks to pass during a game against the Missouri Tigers at Kyle
Field on November 24, 2012 in College Station, Texas. *Getty Images.*

Printed in the United States

10 9 8 7 6 5 4 3 2 1

CONTENTS

PREFACE

A GRAND TEMPTRESS from the past, motion picture star Bette Davis, said it best. Old age ain't for sissies.

I am an old man. No. There's a better, more apt designation for people such as myself: Old Fart. The person who coined that simple term devised it for me. Not only am I an annual starter in the all-star game in the Old Fart League, but it seems a certainty that I rate shoo-in status to be recognized with an Old Fart Lifetime Achievement Award at the Golden Years Oscar presentations that are conducted annually somewhere in Florida.

Everyone who knows me says so. The acceptance speech has already been prepared. Thank you! Thank you! First, let me express my appreciation to the Academy for . . . wait. I can't find my glasses. How do they expect to me to read this crap without my glasses? Goddamnit. That really pisses me off.

That is the prime attribute that's found in these Old Fart Hall of Famers. They are always pissed off. Everything pisses them off. It does me, anyway. Politics pisses me off. Well, that really should not qualify because politics pisses everybody off.

Traffic pisses me off. Not the garden variety gridlock that happens on the freeways during rush hour. It's that incessant crosstown traffic that happens when those late-to-work jerk-offs stuck in the gridlock freak out and look for some shortcut, always directly through my neighborhood. Stupid sons-a-bitches. They really piss me off. When God finally sobers up and appoints me Emperor of the Planet, those pop-dicks, always driving SUVs and going twenty miles over the speed limit, will be the first ones to face the firing squad.

Come to think of it, though, speed limits piss me off, too. Particularly the school zone kind. The nearest outlet to my house that sells hard liquor is four school zones away! Imagine how pissed off I get at the notion of slowing down to twenty miles an hour every half-mile during mid-afternoon en route to securing a pint of Jim Beam.

Elderly people, as opposed to Old Farts (there's a big difference), piss me off worst, particularly in the grocery store. You know the ones . . . those doddering bags of grave dust who get in line right in front of you at the cash register, the ones who've got the shakes so it takes 'em half the day to fish nineteen cents out their chickenshit little change purses.

What pisses me off most is how much younger people resent Old Farts. One time I overheard two of them, girls that is, discussing the topic. "I just can't stand when some old guy comes on to me. Gives me the creeps. They all have this kind of—smell," one of them said.

"Like what?" said her friend.

"I dunno," the other one came back. "Kinda like, uh, furniture polish."

Talk about depressing. So one can quickly guess how I pissed off I was toward the end of the summer in 2012 when my neck went totally nuts after I'd tried to lift something heavy out of the trunk of the Grand Marquis. It started out bad and only got worse. Finally, in utter despair, not long after daylight on a Saturday, I headed for the ER at Medical City Hospital on Forest Lane in North Dallas desperate for some kind—any kind—of relief. This was the same hospital where Larry Hagman, better known to the world as J. R. Ewing, would die just a couple of months later. Crosstown traffic, on my Saturday morning of unmitigated despair, was god-awful as usual, and my blood was boiling like McDonald's coffee.

This was the first time I'd ventured into Medical City since I got married there in 1986. The U.S. district judge who had agreed to perform the ceremony back then was in there vainly trying to recuperate from a respiratory crisis. He thought it would be a fun idea to finalize the nuptials in his hospital room. To this day, I'm the only person I've ever heard of who was married in a hospital. Medical City got word of the event and sprung for a bottle of champagne.

On this subsequent visit, they weren't quite as cordial. Persons who work at the admission desks at ER facilities are rigorously trained in the high art of passive aggression. Finally, they let me in. This slick young doctor from Iran or Albania some sorry-ass place like that surveyed the form I'd completed. "Oh ho!" he said, acting jolly. "You're seventy years old! How did that happen?"

"Sure as hell wasn't my idea," I shot back. The guy really pissed me off.

He ordered a CAT scan, and the results were worded in all of this MD lingo that translated into, "You call that a neck? You'd be better off dead." A nurse entered the room and hooked me up to an IV, and then injected something into the tube.

"What's that?" I inquired.

"Morphine," she said.

Ohhh boy, did I love the sound of that! *Morphine* is a beautiful word, a lovely word that rolls off the tongue, like *sapphire*, or *orgasm*, or *tapioca*. The stuff kicked in, and suddenly I wasn't as pissed off. In fact, it was hard to recall a situation in recent years when I felt less pissed off. The nurse asked whether I wanted to watch some TV. As a matter of fact, I sure did.

One of the surviving simple pleasures that exist for guys who are experiencing the fourth quarter of the game of life consists of watching, in moderation, selected sports events on TV. An attraction that day was something clearly worthy of attention from any sports fan in Texas: the Texas Aggies were finalizing their divorce from competition within the Lone Star State and making their world premiere in the football jungles of the Southeastern Conference. They had quit the Big 12 in what every Joe Six-Pack fan in the state regarded as a simple act of self-destruction.

Anyone who ever watched a college football game realized what a bad-ass league that was. Nobody compared. SEC players were bigger, faster, and meaner than anything anywhere in the rest of the land, and I can say that without fear of contradiction. The reason for this regional superiority comes down to basic nutrition. Turnip greens are better for you than pasta; possum belly offers vastly more vitamin enrichment than beef steak. So it naturally follows that these Southern kids grow up with happier and healthier bodies than kids in the grease-drenched Rust Belt and certainly those poor folks on the Left Coast who are subjected to all of that organic crap.

In fact, those SEC players are so healthy that they're dangerous. The Department of Homeland Security should position men armed with tranquilizer guns along the sidelines of SEC football games. It seems inevitable, only a matter of time, before one those players goes berserk, leaps into the stands, and starts snapping the heads off harmless spectators.

This was the dangerous world that awaited the Texas Aggies in all of their innocence. And they probably could not have selected a more threatening opponent for their maiden voyage—the University of Florida. Natural-born killers from the swampland. Ball carriers had been known to charge head-on into the Florida defense and then vanish forever, the only remaining trace being a loud burp from a linebacker. The Aggies would be served up as gator bait.

So Florida kicked off, and something completely unforeseen happened. The Aggies' offense ran onto the field led by this freshman quarterback named Johnny Manziel, wearing No. 2, the product of a remote community situated deep in the Texas outback. Manziel qualified as a rank unknown, and the Florida defense must have been casually measuring him for a shallow grave. But what do you know? The Gators couldn't tackle him.

Manziel whipped and dipped and zigged and zagged and left those Florida goons grasping at thin Texas air. Plus, his passes were delivered with a hair-trigger release. I couldn't believe what I was watching. The guy performed like some digitally created superhero on a movie screen. Oh, wait. It must have been a mirage, some kind of morphine-induced hallucination. That's what it was. But hallucination or not, the score that was posted at halftime on the screen confirmed that the Aggies were ahead, and the announcer kept on gushing about Manziel this and Manziel that.

Then the nurse materialized and asked if I might need some more morphine.

Well . . . as long as you're up . . .

The remainder of the afternoon promptly faded from any semblance of reality and into a dream state. Soon I was completely immersed in Happyland, and I was transported back to my childhood, when my favorite thing to do was watch college football. That was in Fort Worth, Texas, in the 1950s, and the home team was known as the TCU Horned Frogs. Kids under twelve, or maybe it was sixteen, could sit in the north end zone at Amon Carter Stadium for fifty cents. If the game was not a sellout, and that was usually the case, you could sneak up into the sideline stands and get a better seat.

The Frogs, under coach Abe Martin, were good in that era. Damn good. In 1954, Penn State came to Fort Worth and the Nittany Lions squad included the first two African-American players to perform at Amon Carter Stadium: Roosevelt Grier and Lenny Moore, for God's sake. And TCU beat 'em 20–7 in a game that was not really that close at all. You can look it up. *Sports Illustrated* published a feature about the Southwest Conference and ordained it the Realm of Honest Abe. That was entirely appropriate, because Martin offered a presence that could only be described as Lincolnesque.

The following season, 1955, the Frogs fielded the best team Coach Martin would produce. They went 9–1, and I watched from the end zone (the place was sold out for sure that day) when they lost that one game. The team that beat TCU was Texas A&M, coached by Bear Bryant. I have to say, those Aggies made a hell of an impression on me that day. They were, as they say in Texas, tougher than a bus station steak. The score was Texas A&M 19, TCU 16. You can look that up, too.

In the following decade, I was fortunate enough to thoroughly immerse myself in the universe of college football. I got a job as a sportswriter at the *Fort Worth Press* (may it rest in peace) and watched games not from the end zone of Amon Carter Stadium but from the press boxes of some of the most venerable houses of worship in the entire realm of American college sports. Sportswriters from the *Press* traveled on the team charter, which was always a four-engine Lockheed prop jet. In 1966, I went with the team to Lincoln, Nebraska, where I watched TCU players steal almost every item on the shelves of the little gift shop in the lobby of the Cornhusker Hotel. The following week, the team flew to Columbus, Ohio, to confront Woody Hayes and the Buckeyes. The massive, glorious, double-decked horseshoe stadium presented a spectacle value that was unrivaled in American athletics at the time.

Some Buckeye was apparently running the opening kickoff back for a touchdown, while the crowd created a thundering din that echoed seemingly throughout the Midwest. But the runner fumbled the ball away at the TCU one-yard line and the thunder subsided. Ohio State finally won, 14–7. Feel free to look it up. The great Abe Martin, it was later revealed, suffered some kind of cardiac event on that trip and would retire at the end of the season.

Tough time for Abe, but I was experiencing one hell of a good time. A major contributor to this dream job was the TCU sports information director, Jim "Hoss" Brock, a relentlessly congenial little fireplug of a man. His nickname was derived from the fact that he that never remembered anyone's name, thus upon each human encounter, Brock would grin and declare, "Hey, hoss, good to see ya." He even called his wife "hoss." Never in the annals of the occupation have sportswriters encountered a truer friend than Brock; he always made dead sure that their glasses were perpetually overflowing. This gentleman was, without question, the greatest PR man of all time. Everyone loved him.

A final journey in that football season of 1966 took the Horned Frogs to Alabama to face the Tigers of Auburn University. The team hotel was in nearby Columbus, Georgia, home of Fort Benning and the renowned 101st Airborne Division. For pre-game kicks, the visiting press corps, which consisted of me, Brock, and a photographer from the *Fort Worth Star-Telegram*, drifted across the state line to Phenix City, Alabama, an anything-goes bastion of lawlessness and vice where law enforcement personnel who could not mind their own business were routinely blown up. The beat reporter for the *Star-Telegram*, Dick Moore, stayed put back in Columbus because he was . . . well, he was a Christian.

Phenix City nightlife featured a couple of roadhouse-style bistros that radiated a genuine aura of human corruption. These were Jim Brock's kinds of places. "I got a feeling we're gonna get laid tonight, Hoss!"

Inside, the joint was teeming with, surprisingly enough, young German women. They had been imported into the area by paratroopers from Fort Benning during overseas tours. The GIs, upon returning the state, had realized they were not as lovesick as they'd thought and had each promptly ditched their *fräulein*.

Jim Brock immediately attached his attention to a Rhineland cutie, an unfortunate choice in that not only was she still married, but her husband, a six-foot-five master sergeant, was present in the nightclub. After Brock had completed a groping turn on the dance floor with the girl, he was confronted by none other than GI Joe. He lifted Brock up by his purple-and-white striped necktie, Brock's feet dangling unhappily off the ground, and said, "I understand they call you Hoss."

The Auburn Tigers, led by coach Ralph "Shug" Jordan (the stadium is now partially named in his honor), beat TCU 21–0 the following afternoon. Hoss didn't care. He felt lucky to climb aboard the charter and get the hell out of the Heart of Dixie in one piece. "For God's sake, don't tell anybody about Phenix City," he implored me. I've upheld that pledge until now.

My college football experience, a time of ceaseless joy, continued for the next five or six years. Purdue. Iowa. Wisconsin. Miami. Washington, Ohio State again (that time TCU lost 62–0). LSU. Georgia Tech twice. On that second visit to Atlanta, a midnight knock on my hotel room door turned out to be a solicitation from an African-American hooker who introduced herself as Cookie. I politely declined, since I was deeply watching Marlon Brando star in One-Eyed Jack on the late show. But I gave Cookie a hot lead and sent her to the room that a *Star-Telegram* photographer was sharing with Dick Moore. The photographer thanked me profusely the following morning.

My final excursion into college football heaven happened in 1971. Penn State. That was one of Joe Paterno's best teams, featuring the talents of Franco Harris, among others. The night before the game, I won twenty dollars off the Horned Frogs' head coach, Jim Pittman. Next day, the Frogs played a surprisingly competitive game and were tied with the Lions deep into third quarter. Afterward, I asked a TCU player who'd run a couple of kicks back for TDs if perhaps Penn State had regarded the Frogs a bit too lightly.

"Yeah, man. Most definitely," he said. "Texas Christian. They thought we were some kind of motherfuckin' Bible school."

The following Saturday night, Halloween, 1971, TCU rode down to Waco to play Baylor. In the second quarter, Jim Pittman, the coach, dropped dead of a heart attack. So for me, suddenly it was time to turn out the lights because the college football party was finally over. I switched newspapers and started covering Texas Rangers baseball.

Still, those memories are the kind that linger eternally and remain the reason why I was never able to shed my addiction to college football. And just when I thought I had seen it all, this Johnny Manziel—the player soon to be known as Johnny Football—emerged onto the scene and produced a magic show unsurpassed by anything ever previously witnessed by these tired old eyes. His performance against Alabama in 2012, when he led the Aggies to huge upset over the number-one team in the country, defied the laws of physics. He topped that against Oklahoma in the Cotton Bowl, and the next season, his encore against the Crimson Tide (though in a losing effort) topped anything he had done before. From my perspective, Johnny Football's performances seemed just as fantastic and unbelievable under the influence of Bud Lite as they had been on morphine.

He did it every week, too, for two glorious autumns, and produced the finest element of television entertainment that TV could possibly provide, and that includes *Breaking Bad*.

Johnny Football's college career ended too soon for my liking. Inevitably he declared for the NFL draft after only two seasons in Aggieland. He'll certainly never play college football again.

As an Old Fart, that pisses me off. I hate the pros.

PRELUDE

GIG 'EM

"Elvis has entered the building."
—Texas music legend Robert Earl Keen after watching the
gridiron exploits of Johnny Manziel

IN A PECULIAR SENSE, the dramatic changes in the American lifestyle dynamic that occurred during the previous one hundred years can be mirrored in the evolution of the demeanor and psyche of men immersed in an occupation that is totally unique to the USA: the college football coach.

The sport, in its infancy, brought forth individuals who were, in varying proportions, showmen, hucksters, political stump orators, and—in a few isolated cases—leaders of men. Their rank and file largely consisted of characters with nicknames like Soapy and Rockhead who were regarded as eccentrics, a word that translates into "nutcases." Some rose above the cast. Take, for example, John Heisman. A trophy named in his honor will be frequently mentioned later in this narrative. Heisman's coaching career at Georgia Tech was a moonlighting proposition; his day job was that of a professor specializing in the works of William Shakespeare, and he was considered one of the nation's leading scholars on that topic.

Pop Warner, whose identity resonates to this day as the namesake of modern-day youth football leagues, coached at the Carlisle Indian Institute in Pennsylvania over a century ago. The *real* man bore scant resemblance to the character portrayed by actor Charles Bickford in the motion picture *Jim Thorpe—All American*. Pop, who wasn't much older than his Native American football players, was what is contemporarily known as an addictive gambler. He enrolled in college three years later than he should have because he had lost his tuition funds—a gift from his father—in a card game. Under Pop's leadership, Carlisle Indians who performed exceptionally well on Saturday might find a shiny silver dollar inside one of their football shoes upon reporting to practice the following Monday. Historians have asserted that Pop Warner wagered on the outcome of Carlisle games, and the program that Warner operated at Carlisle would, in today's world, probably have received a lifetime suspension from the National Collegiate Athletic Association.

Nobody in the early stages of the sport, of course, could surpass the exploits of Knute Rockne of the Notre Dame Fighting Irish. Through the fog and smoke that inevitably obscures the true details of the past, the question "Myth or legend?" enshrouds the Rockne legacy. While it is undeniably true that Notre Dame innovated a concept known as the forward pass in a game in which Rockne was an actual player, did he actually invent the play? Was his "win one for the Gipper" halftime speech—the greatest example of oratory since the Gettysburg Address—actually an after-the-fact event co-scripted with sportswriter and literary genius Grantland Rice? Did he actually design a portion of his offense around the tactical formations seen displayed by chorus-line dancers in a Broadway musical? Maybe so. Maybe not. The issue that matters is that these tales ingrain Rockne as one of the great characters in the American tapestry of his time, ranking up there with Babe Ruth and Harry Houdini, and he permanently established the identity of the college football coach as a figure of celebrity importance.

During the post–World War II era, when the sport erupted into a prominence that rivaled major-league baseball, a different breed of coach began to emerge. These *were* the leaders of men—part battlefield commander, part boot camp drill sergeant, the kind of guy with whom the so-called Greatest Generation closely identified. Colonel Earl "Red" Blaik at West Point, when the Black Knights of the Hudson rendered wholesale devastation on most foes, presented a sideline persona that could not be separated from that of supreme commander Douglas MacArthur.

Far more than the rich guys and politicians of the era, Blaik and Lahey and some other contemporaries were the trademark leadership figures of what now should be recalled as the "do as you are told" generation.

Their breed morphed into heartier and more charismatic personalities who were hip to the concept of media. Paul "Bear" Bryant, first at Kentucky, then at Texas A&M, and finally at Alabama, came packaged with the most don't-fuck-with-me ambiance of any figure in the annals of sport—or anything else. Bud Wilkinson at Oklahoma was a master strategist, motivator, and promoter of the ethics of wholesomeness, clean living, and straight thinking. Wilkinson was the first and only college football coach to appear in a national television ad, in which he informed the nation that his boys prevailed in forty-seven straight games because they were fortified each morning with a bowl of Quaker oatmeal. The Bryants and the Wilkinsons were not merely role models who commanded respect. Among their "political base," they were worshipped.

Then there was Woody Hayes at Ohio State, who must be characterized, and accurately so, as the last of his species. Hayes, who was about as lovable as Josef Stalin, didn't give a damn about his image and went about his business doing things "his way" because he realized that the people who signed his paychecks were scared shitless of him. He was perpetually true to the impression that he wished to piss on everyone he encountered, which gave him all of the warmth and charm of a pit bull with hemorrhoids. Hayes once chastised one of his teams at the halftime of an opener at Columbus, shouting at the kids because they "were jumping around like a bunch of goddamn pansies." He would eventually be done in by what he regarded as a collapse of the American moral ethos, otherwise known as the sixties.

As a motivating tactic, his ritual involved taking the entire team to a movie every Friday night before a game. The genre would always be the same—either a war movie or a Wild West shoot-'em-up show. Then came the fateful occasion when Hayes and the Buckeyes went to see *Easy Rider*. Hayes thought it was supposed to be a western—not some blasphemous opus glorifying hippies. "That did it," he told an interviewer for a BBC documentary about American college football. "That *Easy Rider*. It upset the boys, and the next day, we lost the game."

Beautiful Woody. The men in the suits at Ohio State eventually worked up the guts to fire Woody for simply being himself. That occurred after a Gator Bowl game during which he punched a Clemson player for having the sheer audacity to intercept a Buckeye pass.

So the Woody Hayes mold was forever retired and ultimately replaced by coaches of the modern breed. They are entirely emblematic of today's American ruling class—the investment banker, the CEO, the hedge-funder—their faces perpetually emblazoned with a phony, thin half-smile that says, "Everything is under control." Many of them sport white visors on the sideline, the kind that Arnold Palmer used to fling into the gallery after sinking the putt that won the U.S. Open.

There are two archetypes of this identity that stand out above all the rest. One is Bob Stoops at Oklahoma, and the other is Nick Saban at Alabama. Both of those teams wear crimson, a necktie adornment much embraced in corporate boardrooms and U.S.

Senate subcommittee hearings as the ultimate power color. Stoops and Saban perpetually exude that sense of power as they stand, arms folded, on the sideline, seemingly somewhat amused and slightly bored. They can get away with it because their teams, except upon the rarest of occasions, stomp the crap out of anybody foolish enough to stumble into the paths of their respective juggernauts.

As the afternoon shadows gave way to darkness and the geese were migrating southward in the late autumn of 2012, something remarkable occurred that people said would never be done, like breaking Joe DiMaggio's fifty-six-game hitting streak. This Johnny Manziel kid, a freshman quarterback straight out of Nowheresville, strolled into the very citadel of college football—Tuscaloosa, Alabama—and slapped Nick Saban's arrogant smirk all the way across the state line and into Georgia.

The Crimson Tide, defending national college football champions and the unquestioned number-one team in the nation, was stunned, beaten by some rustic intruders from Texas A&M. The Aggies were embarking on their inaugural season in the Southeastern Conference, having migrated over from the Big 12. These SEC neophytes were not exactly regarded as wedding crashers, but more like distant relative invitees who really didn't belong. The Aggies won, 29–24, by the inspired playing of Johnny Manziel. The Tide couldn't stop him, and, in truth, the Aggies dominated the game to an extent that the final score did not represent.

Afterward, Nick Saban was almost speechless. According to one crass media observer, Saban's face was "puckered up like a chicken's asshole."

Act II, orchestrated and produced by the player who was now being described as an overnight Roman candle and nationally recognized as "Johnny Football," outdid the Alabama showing. Having won the Heisman Trophy, Johnny Football and his Aggie companions faced one final on-the-field challenge. That was against—guess who?—the supremely confident Bob Stoops and his kingly Oklahoma Sooners in the post–New Year's Cotton Bowl Classic. The game was scheduled at the massive Cowboys Stadium in Arlington, Texas, that featured a video screen the size of North Dakota. Heisman in hand, Mr. Football was obligated then to live up to the hype, and there was plenty.

Stoops' game face could not be written off as a smirk. He conducted himself with an "I'm the brightest guy in the room" swagger that was permanently set in place in October 2000, when the Sooners beat Texas, 63–17, in a matchup that is regarded by many as the fiercest rivalry in college football. People in Oklahoma certainly think that it is, anyway, and that monster blowout in '00 will be remembered by tens of thousands of OU loyalists as the happiest day of their lives.

Stoops' too-cool-for-school stage presence was permanently etched into boilerplate in 2003 on a Texas A&M day of infamy. That day, Oklahoma beat the Aggies 77–0, and the whole time, Stoops paced the sideline like a man trying hard to keep from busting out laughing, kind of like an adult amidst children, watching a Three Stooges rerun and thinking, "This is really stupid, but still, it's entertaining as hell."

During the week of interviews leading up to the game, Stoops maintained body posture that seemed to subtly suggest, "Johnny Football, huh? Well, he'll have to run that past me first."

At 10:21 CST, in the early minutes of the fourth quarter, former Super Bowl champion coach Tony Dungy, one of the sport's most astute commentator-analysts, issued this tweet: "Johnny Manziel is just killing Oklahoma. Looks like the Heisman voters got it right this time!"

When it was over, Manziel had compiled 516 total yards against one of the nation's most prideful defenses, a bowl game record, and participated in four touchdowns. He could have had more, but Aggie coach Kevin Sumlin devoted most of the final fifteen minutes to running out the clock and holding down the score (which was something Stoops had neglected to do in the '03 slaughter of the

Aggies). By the finish, all of the approximately fifty thousand crimson-clad Sooner fans had fled the stadium, and had the TV ratings people been keeping track, they would have probably determined that nine households north of the Red River were still tuned in to the game. If they had been watching, there would have seen, on the face of Bob Stoops, the expression of a man who had come home from work to discover that his front porch had been stolen.

The final score, by the way, was 41–13, and that made for the darkest day in Oklahoma since Chapter 4 of *The Grapes of Wrath*.

Johnny Football stands out as the perfect metaphor for the unique universe that calls itself Texas. Manziel spent his teenage years in the town of Kerrville, set amid the expansive landscape that lies on the western edge of the Hill Country, amid the realm of God, guns, goat cook-offs, and rattlesnake roundups. It's the kind of town where the locals look at you funny if you don't have a dead deer strapped to the roof of your American-made pickup truck.

It is ironic that Manziel, All-American quarterback with the Kerrville Tivy High School Antlers, had wanted at first to play for the Texas Longhorns. UT coach Mack Brown is a guy who probably likes to crumble cornbread into his buttermilk and eat hackberry pie. He represents a kind of aw-shucks come-on like Sheriff Andy Taylor of Mayberry, and he refused to offer Johnny a job. Of course, Brown also took a pass on two other quarterback prospects from his state: Robert Griffin III and Andrew Luck, the winner and first runner-up in the Heisman Trophy voting in 2011.

All of that serves as merely one of many substantial subplots in the epic saga of Johnny Football. The events of the 2012 and 2013 football campaigns at College Station constitute a genuinely special story about a special player at a special school.

And this is the story.

INTRODUCTION

MOST TEXANS DON'T BELIEVE in the concept known as evolution.

The state's current assembly of legislators is a bastion of fervent social conservatism unseen in this land since the leadership counsels of seventeenth-century Salem, Massachusetts, and it's perpetuating a fiery-eyed campaign to purge the godless teachings of Charles Darwin from public school textbooks.

Where? Show us where the Bible says anything about Jesus and Mary and Moses and all the rest of that compelling cast of characters being the product of monkeys and lizards. No, that supposition completely ruins the plot and any further discussion of the topic becomes meaningless. Never in the annals of human interchange has anyone ever won an argument with a true believer.

Or they hadn't, at least, until the emergence in very recent years of a phenomenon of organic metamorphosis heretofore unseen in the practice of science and theology. It involves a category of humanity known as the Texas high school quarterback. Something has happened to these people, something strange, something otherworldly, something that not even the most stentorian voices from the First Baptist pulpits throughout the state can't even begin to explain.

How or why are these football players suddenly endowed with the capacity to throw and complete a forward pass? For decade after decade, Lone Star football fans might discover a unicorn grazing on the lawn of the county courthouse before they were likely to see a high school football team that featured the prototypical pocket-passer—a.k.a. the pro-style quarterback. Since this place historically goes to extreme lengths to promote itself as TEXAS! THE WHITE TRASH STATE THAT DOES FOOTBALL RIGHT!, the notion that the warriors of the brotherhood of *Friday Night Lights* were led by half-assed quarterbacks seems beyond absurd.

Consider, then, this statistic—arguably the strangest stat in all of sports. Between the years 1955 and 1998, how many starting quarterbacks in the National Football League played high school football in Texas? The answer is one. Memorize that simple number and go win some bets.

You can look it up. (I don't know where, but it's out there someplace.) From the season Don Meredith finished his prep career at Mount Vernon (1955) and Drew Brees completed his schoolboy days at Westlake High School in Austin, a procession that includes about eleven billion signal-callers, only one Texan experienced any measure of success playing the premiere position of the NFL. And that Texan—Tommy Kramer from San Antonio, who started several seasons with the Minnesota Vikings after Fran Tarkenton retired—scarcely qualifies as a Hall of Fame commodity. We're talking about a span of years that extends from Ike's first term and into Slick Willie's second.

It was bizarre, akin to the Harvard MBA program going a half-century and producing one solitary graduate who was able to land a job on Wall Street. Texans with forgettable names such as Karl Sweetan, Steve Ramsey, and Wade Wilson might have started a game or three because the first-string guy broke his leg. None, however, opened a season with a starting job.

That raises the question of why. One presentable theory is that Texas kids lead the nation in the incidence of missing digits due to snakebite and gunshot mishaps. Go try throwing a tight spiral without an index and middle finger. Cannot be done.

However, there is a deeper and more fundamental explanation for the quarterback famine that existed all of those years. It involves a theoretical doctrine that was written in blood and cast into boilerplate within the ranks of the Texas High School Football Coaches Association: for half of the twentieth century, they felt that the forward pass was for sissies. Texas youth were saturated with the notion that no good thing on the gridiron was accomplished without bloodshed. If you ain't into that, then try out for the hopscotch team. That mindset was best articulated by a South Texas football coach in the early 1970s who earned his fifteen minutes' worth in a pre-game pep talk in which he bit the head off a live chicken and then exhorted his student athletes to, and these were his exact words, "Go out there and kill 'em . . . as in dead."

When Darrell Royal, a Dust Bowl Okie, arrived in Austin to coach the UT Longhorns in 1957, he proclaimed, "Three things can happen when you throw a pass, and two of them are bad." Royal would later elaborate that the one "good thing" was getting a roughing the passer call that not only resulted in automatic first down, but if the foul was egregious enough, "the son of a bitch might think twice before he throws another one."

That philosophy struck a chord with every prep coach in the entire state. Real men run the ball, and then they run it some more. So for the better part of fifty years, Texas high school teams exclusively ran the Split T that was modified into the Wing T, and then the Wishbone T, and then the Veer. Thus, Texas high schools presented the NFL with a legion of stud runners like Greg Pruitt, Earl Campbell, Billy Sims, Eric Dickerson, and Thurman Thomas. That stuff is easy to coach. No finesse required.

It was a formula offensive approach that offered a genuine reflection of the mindset of the Texas high school coaches who predominated for a lengthy process of decades. They were known as "character builders." These men generated a substantial and lasting impact on the psyches of literally tens of thousands of teenage boys who were placed under their tutelage. Much of that resulted in a condition of disrepair that can be compared to what is known as post-combat stress disorder. At class reunions, particularly of the fortieth and fiftieth vintage, ex–football players in small rooms talk softly amongst themselves about the horrors they experienced on the practice fields of long ago.

For years, workout routines mandated Rule Number One, and this too was etched in boilerplate: under no circumstances will players be allowed to drink water. The condition of dehydration was apparently something that existed only on the moon. After three hours of brutal physical hardship on unimaginably hot and dusty practice fields, players would stand in the shower and gulp water straight from the spray for five full minutes. Injured players were branded as quitters. The common admonition resounded across the field, time after time: "Git up, you gutless piece-a-shit! You ain't hurt!" On many occasions, the team trainer—always a student who, fortunately for him, was endowed with a gimp leg from childhood polio and exempted from having to actually play—would timidly approach a character builder.

"Er, Coach? Tommy Bob's in there pissin' blood."

"Well, how in the hell is that my problem?"

Once a year, moments before what had been identified as the game of the season, the coach would take on an almost paternal demeanor and deliver a motivational address. Here is an actual, word-for-word example, direct from the transcript, presented by a leader of young men who was sometimes known as Golden Toe because he'd missed an extra point that cost his college team an important game.

> GOLDEN TOE: Listen up, fellas. What's gonna happen tonight is something that you are going to remember for forever. But here's the deal. You might not remember the final score. You might not even remember whether you won or lost the game. But what I do want you to remember is that you went out there and tried to break somebody's neck, and put the sonuvabitch in a wheelchair for the rest of his life. And, if you don't beat those guys to a fuckin' pulp, then God help you in practice next Monday. Now. McGriff—lead us in the Lord's Prayer.
> McGRIFF: Uh . . . uh. The Lord is my shepherd . . .
> GOLDEN TOE: Goddamn! That ain't it! What the hell's the matter with you, McGriff?

Years later, at one of those class reunions, McGriff would reflect, "When you fuck up the pre-game prayer, there's a pretty good chance the odds will be against you on that two-point conversion try right at the end of the game. You know. Looking back on it, it's a wonder they didn't kill us all. The only thing to come out of that whole high school football experience was that afterward, Marine Corps boot camp was a breeze, and it kind of prepared me for marriage, too."

Those coaches were a breed unto themselves and universally could be identified by thick necks, crew cuts, short-sleeved white shirts purchased at Sears, polyester slacks that were a bright shade of red or blue, and white shoes. It was an ensemble they sported year-round, even into the 1980s. Their mantra and spiritual ethos was devotion to the time-honored KISS formula: Keep It Simple, Shithead. Specifically, it applied to designing their offense; the standard playbook consisted of no more than two sheets of mimeographed paper.

Then, circa the mid-1990s, the coach of the Stephenville Yellow Jackets, Art Briles, discovered what seemed an easier path to the end zone. He invented an offense, kind of a single-wing hybrid that looked like something drawn from the playbook of the Harlem Globetrotters. Shoot first and damn the consequences. It worked. They slung the football, and the scoreboard took off like the running total on a gasoline pump. Stephenville became of the scourge of Texas, drawing crowds of twenty-thousand-plus fans toting oil cans filled with ball bearings. They would rattle those things for the entire game and the din could be heard three counties away. (Briles' first star quarterback, Brandon Stewart, committed to Tennessee and started his first game as a true freshman, beating out another freshman named Peyton Manning.)

Stephenville would win state championships for several seasons, the exact ones posted on billboards throughout the town, until (according to a reliable source) the dentist who supplied the players with their steroids was killed in a car wreck. But next to pornography, there is no copycat profession in America that can match football coaching. The Briles template swept the state, and soon the tedium of those "three yards and a cloud of ragweed" offensives gave way to the spread offenses that dominate the sport at every level. Gradually at first, and then all of sudden, the National Football League discovered itself inundated by a cascade of quarterbacks.

In 2013, the NFL QB club found sixteen Texans among its membership. That group includes bona fide starter Brees, who won a Super Bowl with the New Orleans Saints. He went to Westlake High School in Austin and attended Purdue because he threw the football too much in high school and no college wanted to take him. Brees became the leading figure of long procession of the New Quarterback of Lone Star football, the modern-day brand.

The others include:

Robert Griffin III, who won a Heisman Trophy at Baylor under coach Art Briles and dazzled the NFL during his rookie season until one of his knees went kapow. He played in high school at Copperus Cove, which is situated in an area less traveled, roughly a little south and east of Waco.

Andrew Luck attended Stratford High School in Houston before advancing first to Stanford, then to an auspicious future as the first-round draft pick of the Indianapolis Colts.

Andy Dalton grew up in Katy, outside of Houston, led TCU to an unbeaten season and a Rose Bowl victory over Wisconsin, and for two seasons led the Cincinnati Bengals into the playoffs for the first time since the Julius Caesar administration.

Matthew Stafford attended Highland Park High School, a patrician learning institution in Dallas that is its own story. It is one of the wealthiest public schools in the world. The student body, at least some of it, is notoriously snotty. During the 1990s, in a playoff game against Waxahachie that was staged at Texas Stadium, home of the Dallas Cowboys, some Highland Park kids displayed a banner that read CASH vs. TRASH. A bunch of them watched the game from luxury suites that their parents owned and that were situated directly above the Waxahatchie section. Throughout the game, the Highland Park students tossed twenty and fifty dollar bills down into sections beneath and laughed their asses off watching the Waxahatchie people scramble for the cash. Stafford went to the University of Georgia and became the first player selected overall in the 2009 National Football League draft. (Historical note: in the 1940s, Doak Walker and Bobby Layne played in the same backfield at Highland Park.)

Ryan Tannehill grew up in Big Spring, Texas, which is way out west, one stop on the Interstate away from Sweetwater, the point of origin of Sammy Baugh and current site of the annual world's largest rattlesnake roundup. If you think Sweetwater sounds awful, you ought to check out Big Spring. Tannehill went to Texas A&M and was an early first-round draft choice for the Miami

Dolphins where he has lived happily ever since. Word has it that Tannehill doesn't show up in Big Spring very much anymore.

Nick Foles went to the same high school as Drew Brees and, like Brees, abandoned the state of Texas to play college football. Foles went to Arizona and then was drafted by the Philadelphia Eagles. Under rookie NFL coach Chip Kelly, Foles led the Eagles to an NFC East division title in 2013 and will be remembered as the player who took away Michael Vick's starting job.

There are several other Texas products with NFL résumés not as notable but not without merit. Christian Ponder played at Collyville, a rich suburb near the Dallas–Fort Worth airport, then played at Florida State. As a sometime starter for the Minnesota Vikings, Ponder has registered mixed results but certainly has been no worse than a handful of other QBs who have struggled in the Twin Cities in recent seasons.

Case Keenum, a product of Stephenville, where Art Briles began the Texas high school football revolution, played at the University of Houston and then started every game of the final half of the 2013 season with the Houston Texans. His team lost every game that he started, but because of that difficult siege, the Texans earned—if that's the word it—the first selection in the 2014 NFL draft.

An interesting characteristic that most of the above listed football players share is that they grew up in what is modernly known as the Great Texas Earthquake Zone. Over the past decade, a drilling boom has enveloped a vast region of the top half of the state, only this latest boom does not involve black gold. What's known as the Barnett Shale, a subsurface geological formation that contains huge pockets of natural gas, extends across an enormous area that covers much of the northern part of the state.

In order to reach the gas, drillers employ a rock-busting technique known as fracking. Since the advent of fracking in the Barnett Shale, hundreds, perhaps thousands, of seismic tremors have been registered—all of them in close proximity to the drilling zones. These earthquakes are not strong enough to create cataclysmic damage, most of them registering three to four points on the Richter scale. Certainly, they are nothing to rival the grandiose presentations of the San Andreas Fault in California, where people still await the Big One. But the Texas quakes provide enough oomph to cause foundation damage to homes and enough to scare the living daylights out of the people who experience them.

The response of the gas-drilling industry, when confronted with complaints about the byproduct of their fracking activities, is "Bullshit! Prove it!" One such driller called the earthquake hysteria "much to do [sic] about nothing." Nobody in Texas— outside of the drillers themselves—believes that. And probably not even the drillers themselves. So North Texans, who have long lived in fear of tornados and wildfires, now must contend with the threat of earthquakes.

Perhaps the time has arrived for the gas drillers to concede that they are, in fact, the source of the earthquake siege and mount a public relations campaign.

EARTHQUAKES CAUSE GREAT QUARTERBACKS!

Hell yes, it's outlandish, but outlandish is what Texas is and what makes the place so beguilingly and inhumanely and barbarically charming and unique.

The focal point of that PR push, when and if it occurs, will be that the town of Kerrville lies just beyond the outskirts of the earthquake zone. Kerrville has not experienced a tremor as of yet, but its time may come. Until the fall of 2012, Kerrville was known as the hometown of novelist, musician, and humorist Kinky Freidman. The Kinkster, as he likes to call himself, runs for governor and touts a background based largely on the recording accomplishments of his band, Kinky Freidman and the Texas Jewboys. Their greatest hits include such immortal folk ballads as "I'm Proud to Be an Asshole from El Paso" and "Don't Wait Up for the Shrimp Boats Honey 'Cause I'm Home with the Crabs."

Even someone of Kinky Freidman's stature had to gracefully step aside as Kerrville's leading citizen after the appearance of Johnny Manziel, former high school hero with the Kerrville Antlers. After all, Kinky Freidman is a personality; Johnny Football is immortal.

The quarterbacks I listed above, all fairly recent products of the Lone Star State, have an important characteristic in common. None of them, with the possible exception of Brees, can be considered a genuine candidate for the National Football League Hall of Fame. By the end of Johnny Manziel's second season at A&M, some pro scouts were thinking the same thing about him.

Manziel did not meet the old prototype of tall, cannon-armed NFL pocket passer. Guess what? A lot of pro football purists may not realize it yet, but that prototype passer is becoming an extinct species among the ranks of the Sunday football warriors. The NFL has evolved (that word Texans love to hate) into an organization that embraces the smaller, quicker, more mobile quarterback. The Super Bowl of 2014 demonstrated that forthcoming reality with crystal clarity when Russell Wilson of the Seattle Seahawks (the new breed) rendered Peyton Manning of the Denver Broncos (the old guard) obsolete and useless.

After Manziel captured the Heisman Trophy in 2012, there was a clique of NFL traditionalists, as well as a flock of numb-nuts media pundits, who questioned Manziel's size and throwing ability. Many of those critics had never actually seen Manziel play, but that never stopped them from issuing their opinions.

The 2013 season largely served to silence the hyenas. As the draft approached, the NFL scouting prospectus on Manziel read as follows:

Does not possess elite arm strength, but can generate enough velocity to make every throw on the passing tree. Also he can deliver the ball accurately from a variety of platforms and angles. He has outstanding pocket awareness and the ability to escape the free rusher. He has the exceptional ability at extending the play and delivering accurate throws while on the move to both the left and right sides of the field.

Translation: The only thing left to be determined is the identity of the person who will introduce Manziel at the NFL Hall of Fame induction ceremonies in the first week of August, circa the year 2034.

1

WE'VE NEVER BEEN LICKED

IN ORDER TO FULLY APPRECIATE the tale of Johnny Football, one must develop an appreciation for the happenings of the distant past, those thrilling days of yesteryear—the same way that Second Amendment advocates must understand a thing or two about the American Revolution that happened a good ways before they were born.

Texas A&M today is a huge, sprawling, multicultural Mecca of higher learning. Introduce yourself to a random student in College Station and there is a good chance you'll shake hands with a perfect score on an SAT test. Witness the school now and it becomes difficult to comprehend that at its origins, A&M was an all-male military academy—sometimes known as West Point on the Brazos—that required grads to accept an officer's commission in some branch of the U.S. military. Aggieland curricula were geared to the pre-high-tech era of the modern world. "A" stood for "agricultural" and "M" stood for "mechanical," a couple of pre-microchip concepts that just happened to make America great.

We've Never Been Licked was the title of a Hollywood movie released in 1943, and it now lies beneath the stratified silt containing the cascade of productions attached to the World War II morale film genre. After the opening credits, the lettering on the screen read, "This motion picture is dedicated to the thousands of students at Texas A&M who participated in its production and are now serving their country on battlefields around the world."

The cast included Robert Mitchum and Noah Berry Jr. portraying Aggie cadets named Cyanide Jenkins and Panhandle Mitchell. Ample real footage showed the cadet corps marching into Kyle Field's concrete horseshoe while the huge school band thundered out the Aggie War Hymn. Later, simulated scenes depicted Aggies in tents on isolated Pacific atolls, glued to two-way radios patched into the Armed Forces network and listening to the play-by-play of an A&M football game.

When the movie appeared on theater screens, it received an unusual reaction from real Aggies, as opposed to those drugstore Aggies who were hired actors reading lines. Many couldn't stand the thing. They were appalled by it. Dark twists abounded in the plot, which involved a traveling salesman working as a spy for the Japanese. He tried to steal the secret formula for a genocidal chemical compound invented by Aggie researchers. William Frawley, later to attain immortality playing Fred Mertz on *I Love Lucy*, was cast as the spy. His accomplice was a cadet named Nishikawa. There was also a kid who was kicked out of school because it was suspected that he, too, was a spy. Turns out, the kid was a double agent who had infiltrated the Japanese military on behalf of the Americans, and the end of the film sees him sacrifice his life for the Allies. The plot was convoluted and entirely unbelievable. The movie was released in Great Britain under the title *Texas versus Japan*.

Texas A&M administrators viewed the final version, and several were less than overjoyed and attempted to pull strings to prevent its distribution. A latter-day reviewer of film, an A&M graduate, panned the plot. "It starts out as *Leave It to Beaver* and winds up as *The Manchurian Candidate*," he complained. "It's no wonder that a couple of video cassettes of the thing lie unsold in a dusty corner of the A&M bookstore. Do yourself a favor. Skip the movie and go to an Aggie football game."

So be it. Yet one must also remember that Hollywood never saw fit to produce any patriotically rousing World War II morale films featuring the Purdue Boilermakers or the Oregon State Beavers. Where was the movie in which a battalion of Georgetown Hoyas hit the beach at Normandy? Hollywood, at least, was on the right track when it singled out Texas A&M as a fortress of tradition and pride that was and still is a one-of-a-kind place. Not even the scientists of make-believe at the Left Coast dream laboratories could screw that up.

Among American institutions of higher learning, there are no schools quite like Texas A&M. No place comes anywhere close to resembling the setting and the unique—some might say bizarre—personality and character of the school. It was established in the nineteenth century as a land-grant college at a time when almost everyone in the state could vividly remember the Civil War and still referred to it as the War of Northern Aggression.

Situated in the isolated Texas backwoods between Houston and Austin, A&M became renowned as a West Point for sod-busters. This is Middle Earth, and its inhabitants from the very beginning constituted the tightest, most prideful fraternity ever assembled. The school song is *The Spirit of Aggieland*, and by God, they mean it. That spirit infiltrates the bloodstreams of those so-called Brazos Valley Doughboys and, to a person, they are convinced that the afterlife consists of a special heaven where only Aggies can go.

Women were allowed in circa 1960. The enrollment in College Station now exceeds sixty thousand, with an alumni population that approaches one million. But the one-for-all-and-all-for-one aura persists as strongly as ever.

The maroon-and-white Aggie football team embodies what they call the Twelfth Man Tradition. That tradition was established on January 2, 1922, in a postseason competition called the Dixie Classic that was played on the Fairgrounds in Dallas and was a forerunner to the Cotton Bowl. They were playing against the Centre College Prayin' Colonels from Kentucky, who were the defending national champions with a roster that contained three All-Americans. The A&M squad was in the process of perhaps staging a significant upset, but at a price. The Aggies were being battered, attrition was exacting a toll, and A&M's personnel were reduced to the eleven players on the field. The A&M coach, Dana X. Bible, summoned a spotter from the press box and asked him to suit up, just in case worse came to worse. He was E. King Gill, a basketball player who had tried out for the football team but was cut because, according to Bible, he lacked the experience and ability to play for the varsity. He never actually got on the field against the Prayin' Colonels as the Aggies persisted and pulled the upset, 22–14. "I wish I could say that I went into the game and scored the winning touchdown, but I did not," Gill would say later. "I simply stood by and was ready if the team needed me."

Still, on the basis of merely traveling to the game as a spectator, and never having played a down, E. King Gill resides in school folklore as the best remembered and most beloved athlete in the Aggies' history. Because of Gill's symbolic contribution that day after New Year's, 1922, the Aggies' fans in the student section haven't sat down since. Gill's statue stands as a visible feature for fans entering Kyle Field, and the tradition that he established has endured nearly a century and may continue for several more. The state of Texas is known everywhere as a place that, if nothing else, plays damn good football, and Texans can thank the Twelfth Man Aggie crew for giving cause for that reputation.

Texas A&M's victory in the Dixie Classic, now buried beneath the sands of time, was historic in the sense that it literally put the Lone Star State on the national college football map. It drew headlines coast to coast. Fact is, Texas and Texans have, and always have had, a sport like football in their basic genetic makeup. The only sport rougher than American football is Russian roulette with a shotgun. So out there on the flat frontier, a game like that seemed as natural a thing to do as sunbathing on South Beach.

Not long after the Civil War, about the same time football was emerging as a college lad's alternative to dueling, the territory that spawned the Texas gridiron prototype was the scene of a bloodbath. Comanche and Kiowa discouraged early Texas tourism by murdering settlers from Fort Worth westward, halfway to El Paso. Chopped 'em to pieces and fed 'em to the dogs. Tied people to wagon wheels and roasted 'em over mesquite coals.

But Texas newcomers, armed, dangerous, and not at all above scalp-taking of their own, killed some Indians and plenty of Mexicans, too, which was their intent before they ever left their homes deep in the primeval hills of Kentucky and Tennessee. They were Celts, after all, and predisposed to homicidal frenzies.

Then, after almost everybody was dead and the treaties were signed, Indians and pioneers began to mingle. Intermarriage became widespread and produced the Scots-Irish-Comanche hybrid that was fast, ferocious, and adventuresome. Sometimes a perfect storm would occur, DNA-wise, and then you'd have a helluva halfback on your hands.

So a sport as barbaric as football would naturally appeal to the innate passions and competitive instincts of these folks. Plus, the games offered terrific spectator appeal—Custer's Last Stand with a halftime show.

The unique intensity of the Aggies' fan base provided a catalyst that generated white-hot rivalries among their opponents at various Texas colleges. Action on the gridiron was sometimes overshadowed by flying fisticuffs in the stands and elsewhere. This was never more evident than in 1926, when the Aggies traveled about eighty-five miles up to Waco to play the Baylor Bears. At halftime, some Baylor coeds, riding in convertibles, circled the field, displaying signs emblazoned with the final scores of Baylor football victories over A&M in seasons past. Speculation remains to this day that alcohol, more than adrenaline, triggered what happened next. Either way, many members of the Aggies' cadet corps, feeling they had been disrespected, poured onto the field and began attempting to overturn one of the offending vehicles. (Several Aggies later explained that they thought the coeds were guys in drag.) Baylor fans took extreme umbrage to the assault and, according to a Baylor student using the strongest language available to a Baptist lad, "All Hades broke loose."

A high-intensity mêlée ensued in which an Aggie cadet, Lt. Charles Milo Sessums of Dallas, was struck at the base of the skull with a two-by-four and died the next morning. Recriminations on the part of the Texas A&M and Baylor schools ran so deep that competition between the schools was suspended for six years, not just from football but from all sports. No one was ever charged in the death, although some eyewitnesses identified the lethal assailant as a former Baylor football player who was a relative of the mayor of Waco. Aggies insisted that a cover-up was in place, but in the long run, it didn't matter. In 1929, the suspect himself was killed when he was run over by a fire truck.

Those were the days, and it was in those days that Aggie football fortunes experienced ups and downs, highs and lows. The highest of the highs happened in 1939, when A&M, led by all-America fullback Jarrin' John Kimbrough, went unbeaten and finished the season No. 1 in the Associated Press poll. Kimbrough was larger than most tackles during his era. He weighed 225 pounds, and his running style was that of an eighteen-wheel semi barreling down a mountain incline with burned-out brakes. Jarrin' John's Aggies wound up ranked ahead of the Tennessee Vols, who were not only unbeaten but unscored on.

The lowest of the lows happened a year later, on Thanksgiving Day, in Austin. A&M seemed destined for yet another national title; however, the serious underdog Texas Longhorns put the hex on the Aggies. Acting upon the advice of a local psychic named Madam Hipple, the student body burned red candles the week of the game to ward off the evil spirits from College Station. In the opening minute, the Longhorns scored on a trick play—a long halfback pass—and held on to ruin the Aggies' season, 7–0. Afterward, some smart-ass journalist wrote, "Texas A&M surely has the fastest team in the country. The Aggies went from the Rose Bowl to the Sun Bowl in forty-five seconds."

The most galling aspect of that disappointment was that it occurred at the hands of the prissy-pants University of Texas people, hated not only by Aggies but everyone else around the state. In its early years, the UT campus in Austin was nothing more than a glorified log-cabin village. Then, about the time the Aggies were beating Centre College in the Dixie Classic, oil was discovered on some remote West Texas acreage that the legislature had ceded to the state university. In fact, it was one of the biggest mineral strikes in the history of the planet, and suddenly, UT was pig rich. It was like a family of beer-sucking no-accounts winning the lottery.

So the school's regents promptly embarked on a white-trash spending spree. They imported Italian white marble to construct new campus buildings, and they paid cash for instant culture. A thirty-two-story campus library was constructed. The school purchased a dazzling array of knickknacks, such as original Shakespeare folios, the complete works of Browning (the poet, not the gun maker), and the world's largest drum. All of that for a school whose only contributions to American society were Walter Cronkite, Kinky Friedman, and Farrah Fawcett.

Seemingly, people associated with UT began to, as they say regionally, "put on airs." They became stuck up, and it was said that Texans began to send their kids to UT so that they could learn to say, "That's interesting" instead of "No shit?"

Aggies began to (and still do) refer to the UT student body as "tea-sippers," and anybody familiar with the time-honored truths of the situation can understand why. Oh, and one other thing. The coach of the UT team who engineered that big 1940 upset over the Aggies was none other than Dana X. Bible, the same man who was coaching the Aggies at the Texas Classic when the Twelfth Man inspiration occurred. They bought him, too.

The Red Candle Hex didn't simply endure for that single Thanksgiving afternoon. It lasted at Texas A&M for a decade and a half.

The cure came in the form of Paul "Bear" Bryant, who was hired to lead the Aggies out of the football wilderness in 1954. Bryant did that in a fashion that would be neither condoned nor tolerated in the modern framework of college football. He loaded the squad onto two buses and transported the team to an abandoned work camp in Junction, Texas, for preseason workouts. Bear's plan was based on the training methods of the United States Marine Corps, the theory being to break the recruit down, rid him of human instincts such as ego and fear of death, and rebuild the man by turning his intestines from pink to gunmetal gray. Players in the camp recall the experience as being worse than hell. People in hell realize they are there because they had lived an immoral life. The only mortal sin those kids in Junction had committed was to try out for a football team.

Half of them left. Jack Pardee, who had been playing six-man high school football in Christoval, Texas, a venue even worse than Junction, was typical of the survivors. Pardee, who went on to play in the NFL and become head coach of the Houston Oilers and Washington Redskins, would recall, late in life, his reason for staying in the Junction *stalag*. "I didn't have any choice," Pardee said. "What else could I do? Go back to Christoval?"

The ordeal paid off. Bryant's teams became dominant in the Southwest Conference. The 1956 team was unbeaten, and the following season, John David Crow, epitome of the hard-nosed football player, was awarded the Heisman Trophy. Then Bryant left to accept the offer to become head coach at his alma mater, Alabama. "Coach Bryant didn't have any choice but to leave A&M," explained one of his early star pupils at Tuscaloosa, Lee Roy Jordan. "When Momma calls, you'd better come."

So, because of Momma, the Aggies would endure two more decades in which they mostly were *persona non grata* in the exalted ranks of the Associated Press college football Top 10. First Madam Hipple and then Momma. No wonder so many of the old Aggies were averse to allowing women in the school.

One respite during the siege of darkness took place in 1967, a season that, prior to 2012, might have been the most gratifying one in the minds of Aggies born as early as World War II. The team was coached by Gene Stallings, one of the outstanding personalities in Aggie folklore. Stallings had been one of the immortals who lasted through Bear Bryant's Junction ordeal. His face was that of a man you wouldn't want to mess with, like something carved out of an alpine cliffside. Compared to Stallings, Marshal Matt Dillon looked like Liberace.

The first part of the season made Stallings wish he were back at Junction. A&M lost its season opener to SMU, a game at College Station that was moved up on the schedule for TV purposes. Stallings' group blew a 17-point lead and lost 21–17 when SMU rallied behind quarterback Inez Peres. The unique thing about Peres was that he stood, at most, five-foot-five. Ponies coach Hayden Fry said the school needed to supply his QB with a booster chair so that he could eat in the athlete dining hall.

After that came losses to Purdue, LSU, and Florida State—and then, at Lubbock, the Aggies found themselves trailing 0–24 and staring directly into the abyss of a 0–10 season. Then serendipity, or God, or some other kindly force, insinuated itself to write what turned out to be the happiest ending since Cinderella. Thanks to the Cool Hand Luke tactics of quarterback Edd Hargett, A&M roared back to beat Tech 28–24, and after that, there would be no stopping the Maroon Machine.

The next week, in Fort Worth, the Aggies faced what amounted to a toss-up match against TCU. They took charge of the game when All-American linebacker Bill Hobbs intercepted a pass and ran about fifty yards for a TD. In the final minute of the game, A&M led 20–0 and was poised to score again with the ball resting at the cusp of the Horned Frogs' goal line. Stallings chose to cut the home team some slack and run out the clock. Hargett took a knee, only to be viciously speared after the whistle by a Purple defender. Stallings went livid. That, under the circumstances, constituted the vilest cheap shot he had ever witnessed. He summoned Hargett to the sideline and issued this directive: "Go back out there and call time out with one second left. Then we're going to kick a field goal."

The ref didn't see Hargett's timeout signal, and the game ended without the dramatics. The author of this book is one of the few people who know about Stallings' intentions because he was standing nearby, on the Aggies' bench, prior to writing a post-game sidebar for the *Fort Worth Press*. Ever since, Stallings has remained one of the author's all-time favorite coaches.

A&M finished the season with a cherished win over UT in College Station, 14–10, the only occasion on which the Aggies won the Thanksgiving encounter against their burnt-orange antagonists from (get this!) the 1956 through 1975 seasons. Dessert came in the Cotton Bowl, when Stallings' team beat Alabama and the old taskmaster Bryant in the Cotton Bowl.

A classic post-game photo depicts the manly Stallings kissing Bryant on the cheek and knocking the Bear's trademark houndstooth hat in the process. Bryant is laughing. In a happy Aggie locker room, a sportswriter (me) told Stallings that the Aggies' turnaround could be compared to something that happened in the 1930s. The Lubbock High School team was in the throes of an 0–5 season when the coach was killed in an auto accident. Saddened and inspired, the team came together and won the state championship. "That's a helluva story," Stallings agreed, "but I really don't think I'd have done it that way."

The good times at College Station ended with the Cotton Bowl win. The next season (1968), Darrell Royal introduced the Wishbone T and created the UT that became known as the Austin Strangler, and the Aggies returned to their seat on the back burner.

The reawakening happened in 1983, when Jackie Sherrill was imported from the University of Pittsburgh, where he had tutored Dan Marino, to take charge of football activities at College Station. Sherrill's first season was difficult, but his response was Bear Bryant–like. Speaking of their future opponents, he declared, "They better get their licks in while they can, because we're going to be awesome."

That was not intended as an idle threat. Sherrill was simply explaining to the Southwest Conference what, ready or not, it was about to experience. A&M soon made three consecutive appearances in the Cotton Bowl and, in two of them, won the game over a team that sported a Heisman Trophy winner—Bo Jackson (Auburn) and Tim Brown (Notre Dame). Sherrill left due to alleged NCAA improprieties and was replaced by his assistant, R. C. Slocum, who sustained the winning formula. Under Slocum, the mandate was defense—that group became known as the Wreckin' Crew—and the team went out equipped with a "kill first and ask questions later" mentality. Perhaps the best remembered player of that group was the most unique—Dat Nguyen. Dat's mother was four months pregnant with her future Aggie when she fled Vietnam in the bottom of a boat, concealing herself from gunfire. Later, Slocum was informed of a dynamic middle linebacker prospect playing for Rockport, a fishing village on the Gulf Coast. Dat's family were shrimpers.

Slocum was skeptical, worried about size issues. But when he went to meet Dat, he was astounded. The kid was huge. "I prefer cheeseburgers to shellfish," he explained to the coach. "Behind my back, I keep hearing people say, 'God almighty. That's the biggest Asian guy I've ever seen.'" Nguyen went on to become a finalist for the Dick Butkus Award, starred in the Aggies' only Big 12 championship-game win over Kansas State in 1998, and enjoyed several productive seasons with the Dallas Cowboys.

But as the curtain drew down on the twentieth century, the era of Aggie football dominance seemed to withdraw from the stage as well. The decline appeared to coincide with an event that shredded the fabric of the entire school.

Each year, the A&M phenomenon was embodied in the bonfire pep rally that preceded the annual Thanksgiving game against that hated foe from Austin, the University of Texas Longhorns. Students spent most of November erecting a hundred-foot-tall woodpile and, when the thing was ignited, it was visible for miles. Then, in 1999, something occurred that changed everything and broke the hearts Aggies at the school and everywhere. The day before the bonfire rally, the structure collapsed, and students were crushed beneath falling logs. Sadly and ironically, twelve students died.

The bonfire tradition was abandoned. After that, the fortunes of the football team seemed to drift into a malaise.

Following the 2002 season, at the recommendation of new school president, Robert Gates, Slocum was removed as head coach. Gates was a former director of the Central Intelligence Agency, and Slocum's dismissal prompted former Aggie basketball coach Shelby Metcalf to say, "Well, at least R. C. didn't disappear."

During the frustrating years of 2000 through 2011, the Aggies found themselves riding the back of a bus being driven by Oklahoma, Texas, and, at one point, even Texas Tech. But throughout it all, the Aggie loyalists maintained the faith. That is the beauty of the Texas A&M football heritage.

In truth, the Aggies can't claim the national championship pelts of the Notre Dames, and the USCs, and the Ohio States, and the Alabamas of the sport. What they can claim is the more important substance of persistence, faith, hope, and the absolute and unyielding belief that better days rest somewhere ahead, just over the horizon. And it never fails. The very week that the popular and even beloved R. C. Slocum got fired, a woman in Tyler, Texas, was giving birth to a child who someday would be known as Johnny Football.

2

SEC: HERE WE COME

L IKE THE AUTHOR OF THIS BOOK, the Texas Aggie football program would have to experience two divorces before they finally got it right.

The first happened with the split that finally ended the athletic marriage known as the Southwest Conference. That breakup had been festering for years, but when it came, it shocked the hell out of the entire state of Texas. Since the end of World War I, a coalition of Texas colleges, including Baylor, Rice, Texas Christian, Southern Methodist, Texas A&M, and the University of Texas—along with an outsider, Arkansas—had been keen competitors. Eventually, Texas Tech (1960) and the University of Houston (1976) would be included in the family.

It was a fun mix. Each school had its own ritual motif, style, and dynamic, and they coexisted in a cheerful (albeit hate-based) spirit of competition. Every school could cite episodes of gridiron grandeur. The Aggies' have been previously described. The Texas Longhorns rank only behind Michigan as the winningest program in the annals of college football. SMU went to the Rose Bowl after the 1935 season and later produced the immortal Doak Walker.

TCU won a national championship in 1938 and gave the world Sammy Baugh and Davey O'Brien. Under coach Abe Martin, the Horned Frogs thrived on their image as giant-killers. From 1954 through 1957, TCU beat Penn State, Southern Cal, Miami, Alabama three times, one of Ohio State's all-time best teams, and Jim Brown and Syracuse in the Cotton Bowl. Also, for good measure, the Frogs went to Austin in 1961 and beat Texas, 6–0, in a game that cost the Longhorns the national championship.

Rice is a small school in Houston that produces a legion of scientists and engineers who win Nobel Prizes about as frequently as most people take a leak. Under coach Jess Neely, the Owls also played damn tough football. Old Jess had the formal and stiffly dignified demeanor of a Civil War general, operating the Gray side, of course. The author of this book, to this day, can produce a rousing version of the school's fight song, "Rice's Honor." That was because as a fraternity pledge at a rival college, he was forced to learn the song and stand on a chair in the frat house dining room and sing it. He's never quite gotten over that.

Since Jess Neely retired at Rice following the 1966 season, the school's football program has been guided by a procession of head coaches who, if placed in a straight line, would stretch halfway to New Orleans. And there is probably no one among Rice's collection of die-hard football fans, all five or six or them, who could recall the name of a damned one.

Probably the standout character was Bill Peterson, who had previously coached at Florida State back during a time when the Seminoles were not very good. Peterson had knack for messing up his word sequences. Once, on his weekly television show, which was live, his team was preparing to play Auburn and its star running back, Tucker Fredrickson. So the show's cohost asked, "Well, coach, what do the 'Noles have to do to beat Auburn next week?"

"First thing," said Peterson, "is that we have got to find a way to stop that Fucker Tedrickson."

The stunned cohost couldn't think of anything to say but, "Whu-what?"

Peterson looked impatient. "I *said* we've got to find a way to stop Fucker Tedrickson."

He never matched that while at Rice, but if he had, it would have constituted the Owls' premier football moment of the last six decades.

Then there was Arkansas, a place that takes pride in its reputation for cousinly love and thinks of itself, according to license plates, as the Natural State. In charts that measure the various elements of employment, economy, education, transportation, and so on among the fifty states, Arkansas stands at or very near the bottom in every category.

The football team's best years came in the 1960s, and they even won a national championship. But the Razorbacks would be best remembered for a losing effort, the Big Shootout of 1969 against Texas, a game that was attended by President Richard Nixon. Razorbacks fans introduced the league's best-known game-day fashion statement, the red plastic Hawg Hats. Those were finally discontinued when it was discovered that Arkansas students were smuggling marijuana into games by concealing it in the snouts.

Baylor? Not much tradition there. The team's finest hour came when the Bears beat the nation's best team, Tennessee, in the 1957 Sugar Bowl game, but the highlight of that contest was when a Baylor player intentionally kicked one of the Vols in the head and damn near killed him.

Texas Tech's claim to gridiron greatness lies in the simple fact that it doesn't actually have one—but isolated out there in football-mad West Texas, it doesn't matter. Lubbock is really a bizarre place. The people who live there, most of them, don't think so. But it is. Sure, the town contains little dives that offer a bit of honky-tonk heaven. However, the behind-the-scenes workings and prevailing mentality are dictated by a rigorous and unyielding brand of Christianity that takes the concept of "fundamental" to vast extremes. For example, Lubbock is the hometown of Buddy Holly, the singing icon of the late 1950s, a genius. Had he survived beyond early adulthood, people who know a lot about the culture of modern music contend the Beatles never would have come into world prominence, so great was the dominance of the pop scene for which Holly seemed destined. But he was only approaching his prime when he was killed in a private plane crash along with Ritchie Valens and the Big Bopper. The event is the topic of the song "American Pie." It also gave rise to one of the greatest snippets of dialogue in the history of motion pictures.

In the Irish film *The Commitments*, tightly based on a novel by Roddy Doyle, the manager of an unknown rock band bought an old, beat-up ice cream truck to transport the group to its gigs.

> BAND MEMBER: Well, I'm not ridin' in that heap o' shit.
> OTHER BAND MEMBER: Yeah. Those were Buddy Holly's last words.

Holly was not, ever, an entertainer actually of the rocker genre. His music is cheerful and kind of sentimental. The most extreme he got was "Peggy Sue." There is a street in Lubbock that is now named in Buddy's honor (they should name the town after him), but the street didn't get named after the singer until many, many years after Holly's death. That's because the churchwomen of Lubbock fought that proposal ferociously on the grounds that his songs and rhythms were way too suggestive and delivered a subliminal message from Satan himself. Actually, the lyrics of "Rock of Ages" are racier than anything Buddy Holly ever produced, but nobody will ever convince the good people of Lubbock.

The Southwest Conference's headiest days existed in the years between World War II and Vietnam. They were articulated to the fans by radio announcer Kern Tips on the game of the week. He was corny, and the fans gobbled it up. Kickers didn't convert extra points. They made "sevens outta sixes." Broken plays weren't broken plays. They were a "malfunction at the junction." Tips let listeners know a ball was loose on the field with "Button, button. Who's got the button?"

God, it was great stuff, and because it exemplified what is remembered as an era of innocence, it was, of course, destined to die a sad and painful death. The definition of "innocence," after all, is "not enough dough." The league had become too regional, too localized to satisfy the nationwide demands of big media. Arkansas hauled ass to the SEC in 1990, a harbinger of what was to come.

The death certificate was officially registered in February 1994. That came with the announcement that the Aggies, UT, Tech, and Baylor would be joining the Big Eight Conference. Rice, SMU, and TCU were left behind as buzzard bait. Their alumni base was too small, and the football teams played to vast reaches of empty seats. The Houston Cougars were cast away as well, but hell, they were a basketball school, so screw them.

Bitterness and recrimination were rampant. The castaways' main complaint was: "OK. We got the shaft. So why was Baylor included in the party?" Much of the blame was leveled at Texas governor Ann Richards, a Baylor grad. Conspiracy theorists, a rampant breed in Texas ever since November 22, 1963, suspected that the governor had employed political pressure tactics to include her old school in the new Big 12 alignment. Ann Richards entered a plea of innocence and might have added, "But if that were the case, it wouldn't have any impact on my support base because there is not a woman in the world who gives a shit about the Southwest Conference."

The new Big 12, like all shotgun marriages, was never an entirely comfortable amalgamation of families. Among the schools in the old Big Eight, Nebraska, with its coach and athletic director Dr. Tom Osborne, was especially resentful of the Texas intruders. He felt they posed a direct threat to the Cornhuskers' death grip on conference football dominance. His fears were confirmed at the first ever Big

12 championship game. Texas upset the Huskers. How dare they? It was as if these orange-clad boors had puked at the Christmas dinner table. Nebraskans would neither forget nor forgive and finally quit the league to join the Big 10. Colorado (which had an equally bad experience against UT in a Big 12 title game, losing 70–3) preceded the Huskers by evacuating to the Pac 12.

Texas A&M was experiencing a gathering disenchantment with its Big 12 digs, largely generated by UT, and that had nothing to do with on-the-field competition. It all came down to the UT announcement that established its own Longhorn TV network. That could only be interpreted as a power grab from Austin to establish an unfair recruitment (and monetary) advantage over the rest of the league. An unnamed official at the A&M athletic department seemed to speak on behalf of the rest of the conference when he said, "Those UT bastards don't just want a bigger bite of the apple. They want the whole damn apple!"

Watching from afar was a man named Mike Slive, who was and is the commissioner of the Southeastern Conference. He is regarded in some places as "slick" and in others as "ruthless." But, like the idiot orphan, he's nobody's fool, and from his vantage, Slive sensed an opportunity.

What he saw in Texas A&M was a rich woman stuck in an unhappy marriage. He knew that the courtship to lure the Aggies into his Dixie-fied household would require tact, and like all successful divorces, he had to be careful to keep the lawyers from getting too many fingers into the proposition. It was a delicate situation. Eventually, the member schools of the SEC came on board with the proposition, and the Aggies decided to pull the trigger, realizing full well that they were about to piss off a large portion of the Great State of Texas. This was a monumental stroke of change. School president R. Bowen Loftin called it "a one-hundred-year decision."

So they up and boldly abandoned the Big 12 Conference and joined the Southeastern Conference—the Wall Street of college football. While the galvanizing event on the Aggies' annual social calendar—the Thanksgiving game against the Longhorns—was to come to an end, most hardcore Aggies were pleased with the prospect of their new gridiron universe. The truth was that the old Big 12, for the most part, consisted of an assembly of stale biscuits. Other than Texas and Oklahoma, the league comprised an array of schools that offered scarcely anything in the way of football tradition. Kansas. Kansas State. Baylor. Texas Tech. Oklahoma State. Iowa State. And no Aggie could be that thrilled with traveling to Lawrence, Manhattan (Kansas), Waco, Lubbock, Stillwater, and Ames—cities where the only thing more absent than nightlife was day life. Talk about the dreary and eternal flatlands. Stand on a footstool in any of those places and you can see for two hundred miles in every direction. So where's the pre-game blow out? Denny's or IHOP? Want to hook up with some chicks? Well, try the Walmart. Waco is not without its attractions, but how many times do you really need to revisit the Texas Rangers museum? Norman, Oklahoma, has more to offer than Stillwater, but visitors count themselves fortunate if they can return home without being killed by an F5 tornado.

Austin, for all of its alleged nocturnal party appeal, is an overrated excursion. Its famed Sixth Street entertainment district actually consists of about two blocks' worth of crappy little dives that smell like Lysol and feature hideously amplified live music that sounds like an Amtrak derailment. What it is in reality is a glorified DWI trap. At 2 a.m. closing time, the predatory ranks of the Austin police assemble and snatch their suspects. It's like Alaskan fishermen standing on the banks of the Copper River and yanking in the salmon. Victims have included not only a legion of UT football players, but the head baseball coach as well.

For Aggie fans, Lubbock is even worse. All visitors can anticipate abuse out there, but for A&M, the Raider faithful elevate it to a different level. Things started to get nasty in 1991, when Tech fans slung ink into the Aggie section, not wanting to waste any beer. When Tech starting winning some games, the atmosphere went from ugly to dangerous. After one Raider win, students tore down a goalpost and rammed it, fork-like, into an area where some Aggies were still gathered. Two years later, at the conclusion of yet another Raider win, some Tech faithful spotted Mike McConnell, who was Governor Rick Perry's chief of staff and the father of A&M's starting center. They ganged up on McConnell and beat him to a pulp.

In A&M's farewell visit, the night before the game, some Tech supporters snuck into the Aggies' team bus and filled it with cow shit. Southeastern Conference? At this point the Aggies would have willingly transferred to the Arab League, as long as Tech wasn't on the schedule.

Football fans throughout the state, including many Aggies, regarded that SEC move as a suicide mission. How could the Aggies hope to gain any measure of success against an SEC gauntlet that included teams like Alabama, Auburn, Georgia, Florida, and LSU? But the Aggies were eager. Now they were confronting teams that provided *real* football history and a game-day atmosphere that exceeded anything else in the realm of American sports.

Texas football fans, for all of their fervent enthusiasm, are capable of doing other things in their lives. After the football weekend is over, win or lose, they mostly return their attention to occupational concerns—rustling cattle or drilling dry holes or whatever it is Texans are supposed to do.

In many dominions of the SEC, the grid fixation remains a 24/7 365-days-a-year proposition.

Some study in Alabama revealed that within the state, atheists outnumber the people who don't ardently follow college football. Another study, one that examined the modern attitudes of American college males, unearthed this gem from a frat boy at Auburn: "There are two kinds of girls who don't know anything about football," he said. "The ones who want to learn and the ones who don't."

Evidently, in that region, the ones who *don't* constitute a distinct minority. A University of Texas law student was in Atlanta late in 2011 and wound up with a blind date for the SEC championship game. She was a coed at the University of Georgia. "In the second quarter," the Texan said, "she looked at me and said, 'Ya know, honey? If we can figure out how to seal off the left inside linebacker, we can run that weak side counter trap all day long!'"

Way down in the land of cotton, college football remains an addiction that is more escape-proof than Alcatraz, and so nobody even bothers to try. The Texas Aggies were on the verge of the exploration of a whole new asylum. Most were wary, but curious and unafraid.

Meanwhile, it was "Adios, Longhorns. See ya later, Sooners."

At the departure gate, the last laugh belonged to the Aggies.

Question: Why do all those Longhorn fans wear orange to the football games?

Answer: So they won't have to change clothes on Monday when they go to work picking up trash along the Interstate.

Question: What does an Aggie say to an OU grad?

Answer: I'd like the Number 3 combo with a small Pepsi.

3

REGIME CHANGE

L OCKED AND LOADED for a farewell tour of the Big 12 that was surely going to be an affair to remember, the Texas A&M football squad embarked on the 2011 campaign saturated with great expectations. Unfortunately—as often happens in real life—those great exceptions turned out to be the title of some old mildewed novel written by some British windbag and not much more.

The 2010 version of the Maroon Machine had been a gratifying one for the Aggies' community and its coach, Mike Sherman. After a balky start, the team came ablaze with success, from mid-season onward. It was a season in which the Aggies beat each of their annual tormentors—Texas Tech, Oklahoma, and finally Texas. That was the first time the Ags had whipped all three in the same year since they had embarked on Big 12 competition in 1996.

That accomplishment was inexpressibly gratifying to the Aggies' fan base. Mike Sherman was finally being embraced as the savior of the program after being hired to replace R. C. Slocum's replacement, Dennis Franchione, after the 2007 season.

Franchione had been a strange kind of cat in College Station. A decade before, at TCU, he had resuscitated a dead-man-staggering program into something resembling a potent football team. In the process, he located a halfback named LaDainian Tomlinson at some dink-ass backwater high school in central Texas and developed him into one of the best college and NFL running backs of his generation.

Franchione left Fort Worth for the high-combustion job at Alabama, but he was more than willing to leave that exalted plateau to accept the opportunity to replace Slocum at College Station. The thinking around A&M—around the whole state, in fact—was that this guy could not miss. His recruiting classes were laden with five-star prospects that made the fan base salivate. But Franchione *was* captain of the Maroon ship that went down 77–0 on that dreadful day in Norman, Oklahoma, in 2003, and his program never seemed to entirely clear away the cobwebs after that KO punch. Franchione's combined record against the Aggies' opponents that most mattered was 4–14.

If that were not enough to finish him, a bizarre, extracurricular hiccup in 2007 guaranteed the coach's forced evacuation from Aggieland. Reports surfaced that Franchione was peddling a newsletter called "VIP Connection" to a short and exclusive list of subscribers who were serious contributors to the Aggie football effort. This newsletter, ghostwritten by an ex-newspaper sports columnist named Mike McKenzie, provided info that was not available to the mainstream media. Though it was never fully alleged, one might have drawn the conclusion that Franchione's "insider tips" could have been put to good use by individuals who like to wager on football games. Still, Franchione profited to the tune of thirty-seven grand off the publication, which was regarded as a breach of contract, breach of coaching ethics, breach of common sense, and so on.

Mike Sherman was hired as a stabilizing force to restore the integrity of the program. Sherman was straighter than six o'clock and arrived with impressive coaching credentials from the National Football League. He'd been head coach of the Green Bay Packers and was offensive coordinator of the Houston Texans when he was hired by Texas A&M.

His first two seasons were mediocre, but the 2010 surge offered a real pick-me-up to the win-thirsty Aggie fandom. The talent core was returning for 2011, and the quarterback, a power-armed stud named Ryan Tannehill, was NFL draft-worthy. This was an outfit dripping with potential.

But, as Darrell Royal once said, "Potential means you ain't done it yet." More poignantly, Whitey Herzog, the big league baseball manager, had noted, "Potential is what gets you fired."

An early-season game at College Station against Oklahoma State set the tone for the season. This had been viewed as a possible conference championship game. The Cowboys had won the league in 2010 and owned a pro prospect QB of its own, Brandon Wheedon. The Aggies owned the first half, pulling away to a seventeen-point lead, while Kyle Field vibrated to the cheers of eighty-seven thousand Aggies. Then, in the third quarter, Tannehill, who had been flawless, threw three passes, two of which were intercepted, and the bleeding never stopped. Okie State prevailed in the end, and afterward, Mike Gundy, the Cowboys coach who is never afraid to articulate his innermost thoughts, no matter whom they might offend, declared that his team won because it was better conditioned. What a dig at Sherman and his staff.

The next game was against the Arkansas Razorbacks at Jerry Jones' palace of joy in Arlington. Tannehill picked the Hogs to pieces in the first half, and the Aggies, unstoppable, roared to a 35–17 lead at intermission. Unfortunately, the nightmare against Oklahoma State was about to become a recurring one. The arrival of the A&M turnover machine coincided with the collapse of the defense. Suddenly, the Aggies couldn't stop anything. Clinging to a one-touchdown lead in the fourth quarter, and facing fourth down and two inches at midfield, Sherman opted to punt. Big mistake. The Hogs roared back to score easily and went on to win the game. Sherman took heavy flak for his decision to give up the ball, and his critics accused him of being too conservative, "too NFL."

As the season progressed, so did the syndrome. The Aggies blew a late ten-point lead against a not-so-hot Kansas State team and lost in overtime. At College Station, a fourteen-point lead against the Missouri Tigers evaporated, and A&M lost yet again. As one analyst expressed it, the Aggies would have a top-ten-caliber team except for a teeny-tiny problem of being terrible in the fourth quarter.

At long last, the season finally ended at College Station in the Thanksgiving "Backyard Brawl" against the foe of all foes, the Texas Longhorns. This was not only the conclusion of the regular season, but the last renewal, for the foreseeable future, of one of the nation's best and most storied rivalries that dated back to the Old Testament. A&M, and not Texas, was venturing to the SEC, so this meant *auld lang syne*. Oh God, the memories, but those would be all that remained.

Texas, which was having problems of its own because of quarterback issues, entered the game as a substantial underdog. The Aggies dominated the contest through the first half and well into the third quarter. Surely, this would be the occasion on which the Aggies would give the ancient enemy something to remember in this final dance.

And then . . . yikes. Those invisible little demons were back. The batted-down pass that should have been intercepted. The fumble that went unrecovered. The ill-timed penalty. All that stuff that goes unseen on the scoreboard and yet is so vital to the outcomes of close games.

Texas trailed by two points with barely enough time left to mount a final drive. The backup quarterback was on the field, Case McCoy, a poor man's version of his older brother, Colt. Case, who would never be confused with Johnny Unitas, all of a sudden decided to complete four passes out of five and then impersonated a college version of Roger Staubach with a twenty-five-yard upfield scramble. As the scoreboard clock ran down to 0:00, a Longhorn field goal penetrated the uprights. Final score of the final Backyard Brawl at Kyle Field: Good Guys 28, Scumbags 29. *Ohh Gawwd!*

But, as Hank Williams Senior or somebody like that once surmised, the darkest hour comes just before the dawn. Mike Sherman would have to leave. Sherman was a nice guy, but as Leo Durocher once expressed it, nice guys don't beat the Texas Longhorns. Sherman had not won the requisite number of games to sustain his spot at the head of the Aggies' coaching table. But he left the house in good order, tip-top shape in fact, with the talent cupboard fully stocked.

Aggie administrators declared that a nationwide manhunt would take place for someone to take over the program, although they knew full well that the best and obvious candidate was situated nearby. He was Kevin Sumlin, who was doing great things with a subdivision program at the University of Houston.

Indeed, Sumlin was the only candidate that the Aggies actually interviewed. He'd won thirty-five games in four seasons with the Cougars and had come dangerously close to carrying his Conference USA Cougars to the BCS bowl game. His quarterback, Case Keenum, was a touchdown machine. That was the thing about Sumlin. The guy knew a thing or two about quarterbacks.

When he had been receivers coach at Purdue, the Boilermakers featured another one of those QBs who had been deemed not good enough, or more specifically, not quite tall enough, to play for the Texas Longhorns. That was a boy from Austin named Drew Brees, who, it turned out, was good enough to lead the Boilermakers to the Rose Bowl, and later, good enough to win the Super Bowl for the New Orleans Saints.

Later on, Sumlin found himself working as the offensive coordinator for the Oklahoma Sooners under Bob Stoops. In 2003, Sumlin helped develop a Heisman Trophy–winning QB, Jason White, and was tutoring another, Sam Bradford, when he left Norman to take the head coaching position at Houston.

Sumlin understood the demands of the contemporary college game. The old pro from the NFL, Bill Parcells, often said that his ideal quarterback would be a "bus driver." That would be a punctual and reliable guy, presumably sober, who would make all the stops on time and never wreck the bus, or in football terminology, never turn the ball over. The new Aggies coach, the first African-American to be head coach at a Texas college (they wouldn't even let them *play* until 1966), realized that a bus driver could no longer hack it. No. Sumlin wasn't looking for a bus driver. The man he wanted was a Dale Earnhardt Senior, who would blow the doors off every other car on the track and run over anything or anybody who got in his way.

When Sumlin accepted the appointment at College Station, he had no idea who would be pulling the Aggies' offensive chariot. The golden-armed Ryan Tannehill was gone, headed for the National Football League, where he was a top-of-the-first-round draft choice for the Miami Dolphins.

So Sumlin faced a void at the make-or-break position with his new team, and that was unsettling in light of the skull-busting defenses for which the Southeastern Conference was famous— or perhaps notorious. Every player on every team was, in the parlance of Jake Gaithers, the old coach at Florida A&M, a-*gile,* mo-*bile,* and hos-*tile.* Not only that, but most of them were the size of grain elevators.

The coach was in dire need of a stud hoss. But before he had accepted the post, Sumlin had heard some rumors about a true freshman on campus whom Mike Sherman had decided to red shirt, a kid named Johnny somebody. His first full day on the job, Sumlin brought out a video tape of a high school game involving the red shirt. He watched exactly two plays and switched off the DVD player. Two plays were plenty. Sumlin turned to Kliff Kingsbury, the offensive coordinator he brought with him from Houston, and said, "God almighty. I can't wait for spring practice."

When spring practice finally began, the quarterback competition, according to Sumlin's public comments to the media, was a dead heat between this Johnny Manziel and another guy. But in his gut, Sumlin felt that he already had his guy.

4

HERE'S JOHNNY!

L IKE ALL GREAT WESTERN EPICS, with the exception of *Brokeback Mountain*, the opening scene in the Johnny Football saga involves a saloon brawl. Well, not a brawl, necessarily, but a tap room misunderstanding.

It was around 2 a.m. on June 29, 2010, and Johnny Manziel, like Elmer Gantry and about 99.9 percent of all college quarterbacks, was drunk. The setting was one of the numerous campus hangouts in College Station that are situated in a development called Northgate. Strung along University Boulevard on the northern extremity of the campus is a series of refreshment centers geared for the tastes and needs of the vast student body.

These kids need some R&R after another rugged day of sitting in classroom amphitheaters and photographing the PowerPoint displays on their smartphones. So they go to find relief at Northgate in establishments such as the Dixie Chicken (ranked as one of the top twenty-five campus dives in America by *Campus Dive Magazine*), Fox and Hound, Hookuh Station, Duddley's Draw, Mad

Hatters, and others. Growing boys and girls need their nourishment, and everybody knows that whole grains work better when fermented with yeast.

What somebody should do is show the daily cash receipts of these Northgate facilities to Mexican drug lords. They'd drop dead from sheer envy.

Johnny Manziel was in the heart of Northgate when he got involved in a dustup that was actually triggered by his roommate, Nate Fitch. The cops showed up and Manziel was cited for disorderly conduct, failure to identify himself, and possession of fake IDs. Nowadays, most colleges provide fake IDs to incoming freshmen in their orientation packets, but that was one of the offenses registered on Manziel's rap sheet.

Because the accused was a starting quarterback at a marquee program, Johnny became a topic in the mainstream media, a.k.a. the American Temperance and Sunday School League, a.k.a. the Brotherhood of Hypocrisy. They cut loose with the customary harangue. *Get this kid into a program! Oh, horrors! An underage youth sampling alcohol. Only a matter of time before he drives through a red light going 100 miles per hour and broadsides a blond honor student. God is going to punish him. You'll see. It's all too upsetting . . .*

Holy cow. Our mainstream media friends should have been around to cover the exploits of a quarterback named Bobby Layne, an All American at Texas and an NFL Hall of Famer. As a freshman, he was AWOL for the opening day of fall practice. When Layne finally condescended to show up, he was confronted by an assistant coach, Bully Gilstrap, who demanded, "Bobby, where in the hell have you been?" Layne's response: "Coach, you don't even *want* to know." So, because Layne was so good and so talented, nobody bothered to ask him anymore. Of course, that was prior to the Twitter era.

Later in life, after a great college and pro career, Layne got busted in a prostitution sting. He pleaded his own case in a misdemeanor court based on an unusual defense that rested on the claim of "extreme entrapment."

"What do you mean by extreme?" the judge wondered.

"Well, your honor," he answered, "if you set the trap for old Bobby, you're gonna catch him every time."

If the modern media can't remember Bobby Layne, some of its membership might be familiar with another quarterback named Joe Namath. In a now largely forgotten footnote in Broadway Joe's resume, at the end of his junior season at Alabama in 1963, Bear Bryant suspended Namath for the final two games of the season. Namath had reportedly been seen sipping beer in public, a violation of team policy. According to some eyewitness reports, after having his sips, he rode through the streets of Tuscaloosa in a top-down convertible shouting, "Bear Bryant! Fuck you!"

"Joe, I'd love to overlook all of this. But if I did that, I'd have to sacrifice a principle, and then I would have to resign," the Bear told his QB benignly. Bear made sure that Namath was back for the 1964 season, just in time to become the highest paid draft pick, at the time, of any player in history.

Similar episodes, only more extreme and much worse, abound among the greats of the game. Those episodes just never made the papers.

Kevin Sumlin realized that the Northgate wee-hours event would die down and largely disappear the moment that Manziel was involved in his first touchdown. But—for appearance's sake— he dragged both Johnny and his parents in for a come-to-Jesus meeting. Actually, it was a let's-cut-this-shit-out-or-at-least-tone-it-down-some meeting.

Sumlin didn't say so, but he would have just as soon cut off one of his big toes than engage in SEC warfare without Manziel at the offensive helm. Johnny had easily won the starting quarterback job in Sumlin's much-awaited spring practice. In the climatic spring game, attended by a Kyle Field crowd that exceeded the entire population of Manziel's home town of Kerrville and all its surrounding hamlets, Johnny completed twenty-two of twenty-six passes. That was genuine showmanship. So it was etched into granite that Manziel would become the first freshman quarterback to start for the Aggies since 1944.

Nobody, least of all Sumlin, should have been surprised. Before coming to College Station, Manziel had originally committed to coach Chip Kelly and the University of Oregon Ducks, with their garish uniforms—designed more for a Mardi Gras parade than a college football game—and second-to-none offense. At the time, Johnny's dad, Paul, commented, "Oregon is Johnny made over. It's his personality. He likes the bling."

Even in high school, Johnny was becoming the stuff of legend. His coach, Mark Smith, described Manziel as "Brett Favre–like." Rumor had it that he was not actually born, but that he crashed into the Manziels' backyard in a rocket ship, wrapped inside a flame-repellant blue blanket. That was not entirely true. Johnny *had* arrived with some excellent athletic genes. Paul had been a draft-worthy baseball player who had given the second-string pro golf tour a try. And Johnny's grandfather, Paul Senior, when he was in his sixties, could stand in three feet of water in the shallow end of a swimming pool, then vertically jump out of the water and onto the side of a pool.

Much to the dismay of coach Chip Kelly, Manziel developed second thoughts about traveling out to Oregon. He was intimidated by the concept of homesickness. "And," Paul Manziel explained, "he wouldn't be able to go hunting and fishing with his grandfather."

When Johnny decommitted, Mike Sherman and his recruiting coordinator, Tom Rossley, pounced on the prize. Rossley had been around, coaching at all of kinds of colleges and in the pros. He'd been the offensive coordinator at Green Bay and coached Brett Favre and Aaron Rodgers. In enticing Sherman to bring Manziel to College Station, no matter what it took, he guaranteed the head coach that Manziel was destined to become, in Rossley's own words, a "legend." He could see that Manziel had a presence that was heaven-built for prime time, and he knew that it was rare. "Remember Rick Mirer, the number-two player selected in the 1993 NFL draft, the quarterback out of Notre Dame? I was an assistant with the Bears when they selected him. Mirer was the prettiest practice player anybody ever saw. But in a real game, it was like a cloud came over him," Rossley told Mike Sherman.

So Sherman bought in. For that, even though Sherman's last team blew the lead in five games, he should have been voted Coach of the Year.

A week into fall practice 2012, all eyes were on Johnny, but none more than those of the offensive coordinator Kliff Kingsbury, architect and chief designer of the Aggies' fast-paced, no-huddle, wide-open attack. Kingsbury himself had grown up not too far from Kerrville and had been a good quarterback, starring for the New Braunfels High School Unicorns. More important, he was the quarterback who changed the course of the offensive dynamic of the Big 12 and much of the rest of the college football world.

Kliff had been the first starter of coach Mike Leach at Texas Tech. When Leach took over at Lubbock, he realized that in order to succeed on a grand scale, he would have to accomplish something revolutionary. Top recruits were averse to the notion of spending their collegiate careers on a West Texas moonscape. So Leach built a squad of JUCO transfers and put into place a wild and intricate spread attack that no defensive coordinator could entirely fathom. The attack looked like intramural football, and some referred to his scheme as the Alpha Tau Omega offense.

Rather than attempt to stop it, one by one, teams adopted an "if you can't beat 'em, join 'em" approach, and by 2011, the Las Vegas over-and-under odds for Big 12 games were often around eighty points.

What Kingsbury had plotted for the Aggies was a super-modified version of the Leach spread that featured a quarterback who not only came armed with a quick and accurate release, but could also take off downfield on his own like something out of a video game. Another reason for preseason optimism was that the Aggies entered the season with a powerhouse offensive line anchored by tackle Luke Joeckel (who would be the second overall player selected in the 2013 NFL draft).

A lot of these high-horsepower offensive attacks attracted nicknames, like the Red Pistol at the University of Nevada. The Sumlin/Kingsbury offense at Houston had been dubbed simply the Air Raid. A reporter asked Kingsbury what nickname would accompany his College Station invention; Kingsbury shrugged. "If you're good, they'll give you one," he responded. Kingsbury didn't underestimate the man-eating defenses he would face in the SEC, but he knew what he had and couldn't wait to show it off.

Nobody, though, was more eager to see Manziel in game action than his teammates, who'd been astonished by some of his feats on the practice field. Defensive star Sean Porter, one of the backbone characters among the team's leadership and an unofficial team spokesperson, offered this tweet: "There's something special about this kid. U all are in for a treat! TV Johnny coming to a set near u!"

The Aggies' much-awaited season opener was set for a pre–Labor Day weekend Thursday-night affair against Louisiana Tech at Shreveport. Events in the Gulf of Mexico were about to alter that. Hurricane Isaac was bearing down on the Louisiana coast, following approximately the same coordinates that Katrina, the Charles Manson of hurricanes, had in 2005.

Even though Shreveport is situated well inland, the memories of Katrina freaked out everyone in the region; even though Isaac would finally dissipate into a glorified monsoon, the game at Louisiana was postponed until October. Poof. What a letdown. Manziel looked at the bright side and tweeted: "First game at home against Florida. What more could you ask for?"

With the Aggies idle, the Texas football media was attracted to Alabama. The nation's top team was playing its opener at a neutral site, an intersectional match against the Michigan Wolverines at Cowboys Stadium. The most prominent and outspoken member of the Deep South media, Paul Finebaum of Birmingham, would attend in person, arriving at Love Field in Dallas in his private jet. Finebaum attracts gigantic radio ratings based on the fine art of agitation. Nobody is more football-nuts than the people in Alabama, and Finebaum enjoys jabbing them with a sharp stick. In his home state, and throughout the precincts of the entire SEC, he is regarded either as the man you love to hate or the man you hate to love.

Privately, Finebaum has occasional moments when he fears for his life, which is the essential reason that he hates crowds. But more than any journalist in sports media, he certainly knows how to incite them. Not even Howard Cosell could agitate fans—really get 'em foaming-at-the-mouth mad—more than Finebaum. And those Alabama fans, even the most ardent with necks the same color as the Tide's football jerseys and the ones named Booger who like to get blind drunk and go 'possum hunting with a two-by-four, they respect Finebaum in a peculiar way because he sticks by his opinions.

In Dallas, a reporter asked Finebaum about his thoughts on the Aggies' decision to join the Confederate States of Football and how the Texans might fare. Finebaum was his customary diplomatic self. "Come on, people. Get a clue," he said. "This isn't that Big 12 flag football they've been used to playing. Southeastern Conference defense would have eaten Robert Griffin alive. Did you see my Heisman vote? I had Trent Richardson [Alabama] first, Andrew Luck [Stanford] second, and Tyree Mathieu [LSU] third."

The Crimson Tide showing against Michigan did nothing to gainsay Finebaum's assessment of SEC superiority. Alabama tore the Big 10 power into bite-sized pieces. Nick Saban's gang led 21–0 and used the remainder of the evening to participate in what amounted to a nationally televised scrimmage. The final was

41–13. True freshman halfback T. J. Yeldon enjoyed a firecracker debut, but quarterback A. C. McCarron offered an admonition to the rookie, implying that Big 10 football was not, in fact, the real thing: "You can play this kinda ball all you want, but it's different when they turn the lights on, and it's LSU, South Carolina, or whoever we've got." He forgot to mention Texas A&M.

Most Aggie players were at home in College Station watching their home opening opposition, the Florida Gators, play at the universally feared Swamp in Gainesville in a glorified exhibition game against Bowling Green. What the Aggies saw was hardly the stuff to inspire panic attacks. The Gators didn't just look human; they looked sloppy and undisciplined. Florida beat Bowling Green, 27–14, and in the process committed three false starts, three offsides, three delays of game, two personal fouls, one hold, and one illegal substitution. This in no way resembled the franchise that won national championships after the 2006 and 2008 seasons—the teams that featured Tim Tebow, carrying the football in one hand and a Bible in the other, accompanied by forty-six teammates who would eventually be arrested on one charge or another.

Sumlin was watching as well and implied that Gators coach Will Mushamp had employed the slapstick as a ruse. "We'll see a different team on Saturday," he predicted

ESPN selected the Gator-Aggie faceoff as its big *GameDay* featured event. Aggie loyalists without tickets realized that they would secure a date with Lindsay Lohan before they would witness this game in person. Kyle Field, occupied by 87,114 hoarse-even-before-the-kickoff fans, was transformed into a human beehive. The atmosphere was not the clichéd "electric." It was radioactive.

Johnny Manziel seemed oblivious to the hysteria. He directed his team with poise and patience on three long, time-consuming first-half drives that resulted in a field goal and two touchdowns. When he ran the ball, he often left the Gator defenders clutching nothing but armfuls of hot and humid early-September air. The

Aggies stacked up a 17–7 lead, and their SEC world premiere seemed destined to achieve boffo reviews.

During halftime, Muschamp, former defensive coach at UT, informed his players that the quarterback who was making them appear so inept was, in the eyes of his former employer, at best a walk-on candidate to play weak safety. By then, Muschamp knew much better. "When that guy runs, just hold your gaps," he instructed his defenders. "Don't chase him. Let him come to you." Muschamp probably did not realize it, but that was the same strategy that the Texas Longhorns had employed many, many seasons earlier when they cemented a national championship against a high intensity scrambling quarterback named Roger Staubach.

That paid off. In the second half, the Aggies' possessions went like this: punt, punt, punt, punt, lost fumble, punt. The Florida Gators won the game, 20–17. If Muschamp had known, that early in the season, what Manziel would accomplish game after game—with one exception—from then on, he would have appreciated how well his team had actually performed during the second half.

Linebacker Sean Porter was sick about the loss. It was another replay of the living nightmares of 2011. "We talked about this stuff all summer," he said. "This is embarrassing. It's stuff we shouldn't do. We really need to figure out how to win games here."

Interestingly, both Sumlin and Kingsbury remained almost unconcerned over the opening day disappointment. Kingsbury loved his quarterback. "He [Manziel] has got a chance to be really, really good," declared Kingsbury. Sumlin added, "We're very confident in the action Johnny showed us today."

Sumlin did not regard the setback as a blown game, but rather a close loss against a time-tested team that was as good as any in the land on most occasions. No need here for antidepressants. The coach was good at his job, which was football, and he realized that with the degree of reasonable improvement this group was certain to attain, he was in charge of an organization that would be a Maroon beast by the end of the season.

During the week, he endured questions from the media regarding the Florida game and whether he was concerned that his players were reliving the misfortunes of 2011. "I didn't ask every one of them, 'Is this what you're thinking?' Because it's not what I'm thinking," Sumlin said.

The week after the Florida loss, the SEC placed four teams in the Associated Press top ten, with Alabama listed at the top, and a total of six in the top twenty. After the top twenty-five rankings, about a dozen or so teams were listed as "others receiving votes." Texas A&M was not among them.

5

A GROWING LEGEND

THROUGH THE BENEVOLENCE of the schedule maker, the next appointment on the Texas A&M social calendar was an event especially designed to chase the post-Gator blues away. This would be a visit to Dallas, straight into the heartland of the realm of the coin. A journey to play SMU, which, for a team like the Aggies, shaped up as more of a field trip than a road game.

That was not always the case. Back in the early eighties, SMU's Pony Express reigned as "the best team money could buy." The Ponies were notoriously corrupt when it came to offering illegal inducements to recruits. SMU alums bought football players like they bought second homes in Aspen and Vail. They loved to show them off to friends, like they would a new silver Jaguar.

"See that Number 34 out there? I bought that son of a bitch."

It must be said of the SMU backers that they limited their shopping sprees to Texas-only talent, and the talent that they purchased wasn't cheap, over-priced merchandise. Those kids could flat play.

Eventually, the NCAA grew weary of all of that Big D hubris and slapped the first and only so-called Death Penalty on the SMU football program. The college athletic governing body did not just hand down the sentence, they carried it out as well—put a blindfold on the Ponies, handed them a last cigarette, and summoned a firing squad. SMU was shut down entirely during the 1987 and 1988 seasons. On football weekends, the fraternity parties preceded SMU lacrosse matches. It was ugly, and the football Mustangs haven't really been worth a damn ever since. The school remains as robust as ever. It leads all American colleges in awarding bachelor's degrees to grads who are billionaires, as well as other notables like Kathy Bates, the King of Tonga, and former First Lady Laura Bush, whose SMU roommate is now married to Sandy Koufax.

The college was, is, and always will be known as a Greek-driven party school, which is why many grads still believe that SMU stands for Suck Me Unconscious. The Mustangs now play home games on campus at a cute little single-deck horseshoe with ample luxury suites and a seating capacity of thirty-two thousand. The two largest crowds were not for SMU games, but for a couple of high school games: one between Southlake Carroll and Highland Park, the other between Southlake Carroll and Dallas Skyline. They call the place Gerald Ford Stadium. That might seem appropriate enough, as Gerald Ford was the best football player among all U.S. presidents, having started at center for the Michigan Wolverines. Well, he might have been. Dwight Eisenhower was a starting halfback at West Point, and allegedly a good one, until he wrecked his knee after being tackled by none other than Jim Thorpe.

Here's the catch. The Gerald Ford for whom the stadium is named is not the Gerald Ford who replaced Dick Nixon in the Oval Office, but a different guy altogether—just another got-rocks SMU backer who might have paid for the stadium out of his checking account.

The Aggies consented to play a game in that quaint little ball park because they wanted to play in the Dallas–Fort Worth market. When it comes to high school football prospects, that area stands out nationally as the Comstock Lode. On this occasion, the visit paid off, as the Aggies got a commitment from the state's top quarterback prospect, Kenny Hill, the son of ex–major league pitcher Ken Hill. The younger Hill now resides in College Station and stands out as the apparent successor to Johnny Manziel.

While the Mustangs were not a threat to visit the collegiate Top 25, or threaten any team that was, they could be feisty. The coach, June Jones, had once been head coach of the Atlanta Falcons. June was a hard-ass, and his players responded to the persona. The SMU roster included one stud: Margus Hunt, a defensive end. Hunt came to SMU from Estonia to throw the shot put and discus, and being six-foot-eight and 277 pounds, he wound up going in the second round of the NFL draft to the Cincinnati Bengals. The Aggies game plan encouraged Johnny Manziel to continue to go out and have fun but perhaps avoid big Margus whenever possible because everybody knows those Estonian giants can inflict serious bodily harm.

SMU came equipped with a big-name quarterback, too. Garrett Gilbert had been the top high school prospect in the state and went to Texas. As a freshman, he played most of the national championship game against Alabama after Colt McCoy got hurt. When it was Gilbert's turn to start the next season, he bombed. He got hurt, got benched, and eventually transferred to SMU. Since Gilbert clearly was not good enough to hack it in the Big Room, the thinking was that he might somehow thrive as a lounge act.

While the Aggies were being nosed out by Florida, SMU beat Stephen F. Austin, a Division Two school in Nacogdoches, Texas, 52–0 on the basis of ten—count 'em, ten!—turnovers. During game week, a reporter asked Kliff Kingsbury if he was worried that the SMU defense, so opportunistic the previous week, might cause headaches for his freshman quarterback, Manziel. Kingsbury stared at the reporter and said, "We're not Stephen F. Austin."

It was on the field of Gerald Ford Stadium that Johnny Manziel showed the football world that he possessed not just extraordinary but, on some plays, supernatural talent and instinct. He rushed for

124 yards, passed for 294 more, and played a part in six touchdowns as the Aggies cruised to a 48–3 win. Those raw stats hardly illustrate the artistry that Manziel exhibited. Here is a transcript from the play-by-play radio call by the SMU broadcaster: "Third and one. Manziel drops back and he's sacked by Tyler Reed! No! He spins away, running toward the left sideline where he'll be forced out of bounds . . . No! He throws as he's falling backward . . . and . . . it's complete! To Mike Evans for a seventeen-yard gain! I can't believe what I just saw!"

Manziel performed that circus act all day long and would continue it all season long. After the game, Aggie receiver Uzoma Nwachukwu talked about Manziel and issued a quote that would eventually resonate throughout college football. Here's what he said: "Johnny, of course, is Captain Amazing back there. No matter what kind of pressure he is under, he always finds a way to get out of it. Johnny Football. Captain Amazing. I'm pretty sure next week, we'll have another [nickname] for him. He's a growing legend."

No. They wouldn't need to have another one. "Johnny Football" hit the spot.

If the Aggies felt that whoever arranged the SMU game deserved a tip of the hat, then the persons who crafted the next gem were due a standing ovation. Not frequently do the Texas Aggies get an opportunity to perform at home against the South Carolina State Bulldogs from the Mid-Eastern Atlantic Conference.

Surely, the persons responsible for setting up this bout received kickbacks not only from the tavern keepers of Northgate, whose establishments would be teeming by halftime, but also from most of the orthopedists and neurosurgeons (along with chiropractors and acupuncturists) in the general vicinity of Orangeburg, South Carolina.

The Bulldogs, if nothing else, were a courageous bunch. The week before traveling to Texas, they'd flown to Tucson to pick up a big check for a game against the Arizona Wildcats, which they lost 56–0.

Coaches for the overdog schools, prior to these grossly colossal mismatches (which the NCAA has decided to curtail) liked to point out what happened in 2007. Appalachian State, someplace where everyone wears coonskin hats, went to Ann Arbor and beat Michigan before 101,000 disbelieving onlookers in the stadium known as the Big House. There were major consequences for both teams. The Michigan coach, Lloyd Carr, lost his job, and the star of the game for Appalachian State married Billy Graham's grand-daughter. Outcomes such as that, like planetary alignments, happen about once every 173 years. Still, good old Appalachian State will forever remain useful as a motivating tool. "See? See what happens when you get complacent?"

It would be impossible to measure the Aggies' intensity level before this game. It might have been flatter than Olive Oyl's chest. But they led 49–0 at the half when Johnny Manziel was given the rest of the night off after registering 252 yards of total offense. Twenty of those came on a touchdown scramble worthy of a highlight film, no matter the opposition. It culminated in an Olympian swan dive that landed just inside the goal-line pylon.

"You don't see a lot of runnin' like that," Sumlin acknowledged after A&M had cleared its bench and won the game, 70–14.

A wire service report from Spokane, Washington, brought news of an area fisherman who had caught a trout with a human finger in its stomach. Authorities confirmed that the finger had once belonged to some guy with a Norwegian name who had lost four fingers a couple of weeks earlier in a boating accident. The remaining three had still not been located.

"Yeah, it's a shit deal," the injured man reported. "But it beats coaching the Arkansas Razorbacks." OK, he never really said that. But he might as well have. Just a year ago, the Razorbacks had ranked as a top-tier SEC football team. Then everything collapsed in the offseason when coach Bobby Petrino wrecked his motorcycle with his girlfriend riding on the back. That incident got Bobby fired—not necessarily because of the indiscretion but because of the attempted coverup. It happens every time. Ask any politician.

Under John L. Smith, Petrino's top assistant, who was selected to head the program, the Hogs' 2012 season had been a complete disaster, a wipeout. They'd lost their opener to the Louisiana Monroe Warhawks. They had lost at home to Alabama, 52–0, and after the game, the Arkansas quarterback accused the team of "laying down."

The Razorbacks came rolling into College Station hot on the heels of yet another home loss to Rutgers. Strangely, the Hogs were only eleven-and-a-half-point underdogs, a spread that might have been predicated on the 2011 game in which they were seventeen points down and won, 42–38. Arkansas always spelled big trouble for the Aggies and the Porkers were at it again in the first quarter, taking a 10–7 lead. The rest of the game would belong to Johnny and his friends.

The big play happened just before the half, when Manziel speared wideout Ryan Swopes with a perfect heave on an eighty-yard touchdown play. "When Johnny made the call in the huddle, I knew it was time to hit switch and take over the ball game," Swopes remarked. That made the score 27–10 and it soon became 34–10 when Manziel scored on a fifty-two-yard run in which he zigzagged through traffic like a stunt driver in a chase scene.

During a timeout, Manziel begged Kliff Kingsbury to allow him to call a play. Kingsbury relented. Johnny called a running play that went for no gain. "Probably won't happen again," was Kingsbury's only comment. In the process of beating the dog out of the Hogs, 52–10, the Aggies compiled 713 yards in total offense, third most in school history. Of that total, Johnny Manziel accounted for 557. Yeah, stats don't always tell the whole truth and nothing but the truth, but they never out-and-out lie. Kevin Sumlin realized that if that stuff continued, he would have to register Johnny Football as a lethal weapon.

At this point in the season, the Aggies were about to march straight into the SEC minefield. The next stop would be a visit to Ole

Miss, Texas A&M's first SEC mission behind enemy lines. "This is a tough stretch," conceded A&M defensive back Jonathan Stewart. "This is where good teams become great, or good teams become average."

What somebody needs to do is erect a tasteful billboard that reads, "Welcome to Oxford, Mississippi. Set your clocks back two hundred years." This town, situated on the western edge of the Holly Springs National Forest, remains completely immersed in the trappings of the Old South's genteel past. One can also expect to experience a vision of Scarlett O'Hara gently strolling across the campus in a pale blue gown, carrying a parasol. Local gentry refer to their state as "Miss Hippie." Original settlers here named their community Oxford in hopes that the state might locate a state university in the town. It worked.

The concept popularly known as political correctness has yet to entirely infiltrate this otherwise well-mannered environment. The Ole Miss athletic teams are still called the Rebels, and the band still blares out "Dixie" when the Rebs run onto the field or make a touchdown. Ole Miss football is not what it used to be when coach Johnny Vaught kept the program in the top ten, or five, for nearly three decades. Other than Archie Manning and his son Eli, football stars have been in short supply. Where Old Miss has remained at the top of the collegiate rankings is in the category of hottest coeds. *Playboy* and the *Princeton Review* remain in accord on that.

Except that Ole Miss girls do not actually qualify as "hot." They are beautiful, in the sense that Elizabeth Taylor was hot, but Ava Gardner was beautiful. At least, that's what Ava Gardner always said.

College life at Ole Miss is unhurried and takes place within the cool and calming shadows of tall oaks. All of that changes on football Saturdays, though, when the place becomes overwhelmed with a dose of SEC fever and everyone goes batshit crazy. Levels of intoxication that would do honor to pagan rituals take place in an area called the Grove, a ten-acre circle of green lawn that's about a half-mile stroll from the stadium. Aggies who'd made the trip were deeply impressed with the Rebels' version of a good time. Ole Miss has a slogan: "We may not win the game, but we've never lost a party."

Unfortunately for Texas A&M, for much of this early October occasion, it appeared the Rebels were about to win both.

At times during the game, Johnny Football appeared to have left his pre-game supply of rocket fuel back in College Station. Maybe SEC football on foreign turf had at last inflicted a measure of stage fright. Bad things can happen to outsiders who get too cocky for their own good when they travel into the state of Mississippi. Just ask those guys in *Easy Rider*. A&M committed six turnovers in the first three quarters, with Manziel responsible for half of those, and every time the Ags coughed up the ball, the Rebel fans got more and more manic and the old Stars and Bars flapped proudly in the nighttime Dixie breeze. Ole Miss led 27–17 in the fourth quarter when the Aggies took over the ball at their own one-yard line.

Somehow, some way, Johnny Football located the old magic. Performing to his utmost with a hostile audience, he engineered two scoring drives. The game-winning TD was a picture-perfect twenty-two-yard pass from Manziel to a streaking Ryan Swopes, who made a picturesque, over-the-shoulder catch near the back of the Rebels' end zone. This was survival. This was escape. The Aggies fled Vaught-Hemingway Stadium with a 30–27 win. (The Hemingway whose name appears on the stadium wall, by the way, did not go by Ernest. He was some other dude.)

Kevin Sumlin's on-the-spot assessment of his team's performance was that they did not play good football, and that it was a team effort. He wasn't sure that his Aggies weren't cooked when they fell into the ten-point hole in the fourth quarter. "A team gets you into that situation and a team gets you out of it. We never quit."

What the coach did not mention was that for the first time in his College Station tenure, the Aggies had won what was not only a close game, but a real stomach-churner. With Johnny Football directing the chant, the demons of the 2011 season had finally been exorcised.

The overhyped late-summer threat of Hurricane Isaac had not been a destructive event, but a month and a half later, around the Texas A&M football program, the storm finally emerged as a genuine pain in the ass.

That postponed opening game against Louisiana Tech now loomed on a Saturday that had originally been slotted as an open date prior to the monumental task of playing LSU. Instead of enjoying two weeks to prepare for the Tigers, the team needed to prepare for the Bulldogs of the Western Athletics Conference. The task would be anything but easy.

Louisiana Tech's main contribution to the sport of football is Terry Bradshaw, but that was way back when. The name of the school connotes minor-league college football, but teams like that create major headaches for the more socially elite. Now that makeup contest loomed as something not fun at all. Coach Sonny Dykes' Bulldogs were operating at full speed ahead, with a 5–0 record that included a road win at Illinois. So the quick trip to Shreveport, a city where the residents of the so-called Ark-La-Tex region come to buy paint and aluminum siding, awaited the Auggies as something that has become known as a trap game.

Johnny Football was more than ready and recorded his latest turf-scorching effort. The problem lay in the fact that Louisiana Tech came to work in a retaliatory frame of mind. For every Aggie success, the Bulldogs usually filed a response. Texas A&M mostly led throughout, but the Louisiana team, pretending to be the IRS, just would not go away. For the Aggies, and that included players, coaches, and fans, this game was like a root canal—they thought it would never end. When the clock struck midnight, the scoreboard still read "3rd Quarter." For all of his offensive heroics, Manziel made a play that implied UT's suggestion that he play defensive back might not have been all that bad.

An Aggie running back fumbled, and a Bulldog retrieved the ball and took off toward the A&M goal line. Manziel caught the guy, nailed him with a textbook tackle, and forced the ball loose in the process. As it turned out, the play had been whistled dead before the original fumble, but it showed that Johnny Manziel was a football player who could do anything.

The Bulldogs scored twice late in the game, but their effort to tie it finally died when a two-point conversion failed. Final score: Texas A&M 59, Louisiana Tech 57. That was the highest combined total for any game in Aggies history. The previous high had been in a game before World War I in which A&M had scored all of the points in a 110–0 win over Daniel Baker. (That raises the question, who in the hell was that Daniel Baker character? The big dummy. If he'd brought along ten friends, maybe the game would have been a little closer.)

LSU followers maintain a reputation as the crudest fans in college football. They do not bother to refute that. They will sneak into barroom latrines in Tuscaloosa and start riots by posting graffiti that reads, "Bear Bryant was a queer." When the Tigers play Arkansas, their neighboring state to the north, Tigers fans issue this motivational message to their team: KILL THE GARBAGE-EATERS! Students have been accused of positioning themselves atop a ledge at Tiger Stadium and urinating upon the visitors' section beneath. "And those," a moistened visitor once alleged, "were the sorority girls!"

On the other hand, they have acquired a measure of sophistication. Burgeoning scholars in Baton Rouge realize that it's a bad idea to scalp their student tickets on Facebook.

So, with the Texas summer heat grudgingly lessening its clutches as late October approached, College Station girded itself for an invasion of the Bayou Bengals. Windows were boarded up, and women and children were evacuated from the streets. The version of the football steamroller that came to play Texas A&M was a somewhat watered-downed rendition of the team that beat Alabama in 2011 and lost in a rematch in the BCS Championship Game. LSU had a loss on its record, a 14–6 setback to Florida that took place in the Gatorland Swamp. The missing ingredient was defensive phenomenon Tyrann Mathieu, better known as the Honey Badger. According to repeated drug tests, the Honey Badger was better equipped to play for the Rolling Stones than a college football team, and coach Les Miles had with great reluctance been forced to cut him loose before the start of fall practice.

Miles' teams, whose products adorn every roster in the NFL, of course came to College Station with a complete assortment of Honey Badger facsimiles. When A&M jumped out to a 12–0 lead, it only served to annoy the Tigers. LSU finally won, 24–19, but not before getting a first-hand account of how Johnny Football occasionally performs in a league of his own. One writer, after wiping the disbelief from his eyes, offered this description of a typical Manziel play: "He starts left, but the path is blocked by LSU defenders. Manziel hits the brakes so hard, a passenger would have been thrown through the windshield. He reverses his field, slips between two innocent bystanders and dives for a first down." On a pass play, Manziel "threw off his back foot and nailed a perfect twenty-seven-yarder to Ryan Swope that not so much fitted into a tight window, but a porthole."

At the conclusion, one top LSU defensive player, speaking under conditions of anonymity, said, "I don't have a Heisman Trophy vote, of course, but if I did, it would go to Manziel."

The Aggies' gauntlet (there was no other word for it) called for consecutive road trips to Auburn, Mississippi State, and Alabama. That was a task equivalent to scaling Mount Everest on roller skates.

The end of the Aggies' fight song calls for the cheer "Rough stuff, real stuff, Texas A&M!" Was it there? The Southeastern Conference was about to find out for sure.

6

HEISMAN HEAVEN

SOUTHEASTERN CONFERENCE football followers, no matter what the school, possess long motor homes and short memories.

Coach Gene Chizik had done Auburn enthusiasts a terrific favor in 2010. According to the mandates of the Ten Commandments and the Sermon on the Mount, at least half of these people would not be going to heaven (you oughta see what they do inside those motor homes). So Chizik—he and Cam Newton—brought heaven to them. That was in the form of a BCS Championship Game win over Oregon that had happened less than two years earlier. None of that seemed to matter very much as 2012's football campaign entered its final weeks with the Tigers sputtering through a trying season. They had won but a single game, and that was over Louisiana Monroe in overtime.

The week before the Aggies arrived in Auburn, a college town near the Georgia state line that does not have a bookstore, the school president issued a letter to the fans and alums, "sharing their concerns" about the present status of the football program and assuring them that the coaching situation would be "carefully evaluated" at the end of the season. Look out, Gene.

Chizik, after the season, would embark on a career as a radio personality. But if he had maintained the slightest thread of hope that he would remain coach at Auburn, it was severed by Johnny Football in the first half.

It was a slaughter. The Aggies rolled to a 42–7 lead at intermission, elevated that to 49–7, and then Johnny was finished for the remainder of the day. Jordan-Hare Stadium was crammed full with a crowd of eighty-five thousand at kickoff. "They emptied out at halftime," Chizik noted. "It's obvious why and I can't blame them for what they saw." What they saw, as long as they stayed, was an offense from Texas A&M that amassed 671 yards, the most ever yielded in Auburn history.

While the Aggies were dismantling poor Auburn, at neighboring Tuscaloosa, the Crimson Tide was deflating what had been an unbeaten Mississippi State team.

The Bulldogs lost, 38–7, but no disgrace there, considering the game site and opponent. State had every opportunity to reinstate itself as a national top ten contender with the Aggies coming into Starkville—one of the most aptly named towns in America.

Instead, the top ten contender turned out be the visiting team, which settled the issue before the half. With Manziel pushing all of the right buttons, pulling the correct levers, and doing his customary magic act, Texas A&M led after the first half hour, 24–0. The problem confronting SEC defenders was the concept of executing their assignments and covering their man. When they did that successfully, Johnny Football would set sail on his own—and that's when the heartache would begin. Typical was a play when the Mississippi State defense successfully blanked the Aggies' downfield receivers, so Manziel simply weaved and dodged his way through eleven Bulldogs, who might as well have been scarecrows in a field, for a thirty-seven-yard TD.

For the day, Football Johnny would run for 129 yards and pass for 311 more. He was beginning to make headlines for participating in a *non*scoring drive. The guy had become unstoppable. Mississippi State players stood on the sideline in the final moments of their 38–13 home loss, looking like they had just endured a session of electro-convulsive therapy. Afterward, the coach, Dan Mullen, delivered his eulogy: "We played poorly, and I, as the coach, bear one hundred percent responsibility."

Blah. Blah. Bullshit. Bullshit. Somehow, these SEC coaches couldn't seem to grasp that their teams really weren't so bad and that these friggin' Texans (and who invited them, by the way?) were actually that good.

How good? That would shortly be determined because according to the Aggies bus schedule, next was Armageddon.

Kevin Sumlin certainly had established himself as a shoo-in for the SEC's coaching Newcomer of Year Award, if not overall Coach of the Year. But he was finished with the task of using Johnny Football to make fellows like Gene Chizik and Dan Mullen look so dummy-like. The adversary who would be at work on the opposite sideline the next time would be a far more challenging presence. Recently, Sumlin had been winning some high-noon shootouts with the likes of Sheriff Andy Taylor of Mayberry. Now, he had to go face to face with Wyatt Earp. At least, that was the reputation that Nick Saban had attained at Alabama and other stopovers through the years.

Saban was born on Halloween and has been scaring the hell out of everybody ever since. He grew up in West Virginia, spooky enough in its own right, played football at Kent State, and was on campus there on that day in 1970 when Ohio National Guardsmen shot and killed some student war protesters.

He began his coaching career at Kent State as a graduate assistant. From there, Saban would embark on what amounted to a grand tour of coaching assignments. Syracuse. West Virginia. Ohio State. Navy. Michigan State. The Houston Oilers. Each job involved coaching the defense. Finally, Saban assumed a job as the head coach at Toledo. That was always the big challenge, to advance from the relatively stress-free position of coordinator and into the kitchen heat that came with the territory of being the man who was the face of the program. Had Saban been ready? His 9–2 record with the Rockets indicated that he was.

Saban left after that first season to go back to a coordinator's job with the Cleveland Browns, where he would work with Bill Belichick. It was as if Saban had earned a master's degree in football coaching and that assignment in Cleveland would be the one that earned him his PhD.

From then on, he would work as a head coach at various locations, and whenever he moved on it was never under adverse circumstances.

First on the list had been Michigan State, a once-mighty venue that had fallen upon tough times for a prolonged stretch in which the Spartans had been handicapped with chronic run-ins with the NCAA. And in those types of situations, schools never win. Under Saban, the team improved gradually and then dramatically. His last team finished at 10–2, and that included a bowl win. Saban then left to run a stronger program (with a heftier salary for the head coach) at LSU. He won the BCS championship there after the 2003 season with a decisive victory over Oklahoma.

Saban left Baton Rouge to check out the sunny clime of South Beach and life in the NFL. His head coaching tenure with the Miami Dolphins lasted two seasons, and that ended up being one of the few low notes in his career. The Dolphins faltered because their upcoming quarterbacking star, Daunte Culpepper, had not been such a star after all.

But at Tuscaloosa during that same time, 'Bama coach Mike Shula faltered and had been dismissed. 'Bama officials offered Nick Saban the job, and he could not wait to accept. He realized that if this was not the job he had been born to take, it was at least the one that God had told him to take. Alabama and Nick Saban were meant for one another, and the union would become a happy one. In 2008, *Forbes* published an article that anointed Saban as "the most influential coach in football." Saban had become the only coach in history to win a BCS championship at two schools.

The best high school players in the country were making Tuscaloosa their choice destination, and the results were being displayed on the field in an overwhelming fashion. After Saban had beaten LSU in the BCS title match after the 2011 season, Saban complained to a golfing buddy, "That damn game cost me a week of recruiting."

At last, the University of Alabama was being coached by a man who thrived while working in the eternal shadow of Bear Bryant. And, importantly, Saban's Crimson empire remained largely untainted by scandals. At one point, the *Wall Street Journal* produced a report that Saban had encouraged some of his bottom-tier players to quit football and accept medical scholarships to make more room for incoming recruits. If that action had been regarded as a transgression, it was certainly a benign one.

Did Nick Saban own the state? Probably. Prior to a speaking engagement in Birmingham in early 2012, the emcee introduced Saban by reciting highlights of his resume:

"Coach Saban has been the winner of the Bear Bryant Award, the Eddie Robinson Award, the Home Depot Coach of the Year Award, the Liberty Mutual Award . . ."

At which time, a voice from the back of the banquet hall boomed, "What about Montgomery Ward?"

Hoo boy! That exemplified life in Dixie, where Nick Saban was living amidst the high cotton.

So during the 2012 campaign, one that was emerging as perhaps the coach's most promising yet, Nick Saban's true concern, the one game that might challenge the Tide, was a confrontational national championship rematch against LSU. 'Bama was better, but the game was at Baton Rouge, where voodoo is practiced.

Alabama won, 21–17, and in the minds of the football public, the Crimson Tide would reign again as imperial potentates of the college game. Saban, with a hot Aggies team coming into Tuscaloosa, issued his standard rhetoric: "It's pretty difficult not to respect their body of work. We've got to forget about last week [the huge win over LSU]. We've got to move on." In coach-speak, that translated into: "We're going to beat them like (a) a rented mule, (b) a red-headed step-child, or (c) a tom-tom."

Las Vegas' opening line installed the Tide as fourteen-point favorites, and that never fluctuated, not even by a half-point, throughout game week.

Saban managed to inject a little controversy into the pre-game dialogue when a football traditionalist appeared to cast aspersions upon the no-huddle, high-speed spread that teams like the Aggies had been employing. "Is this what we want football to be?" Saban said.

Three days before the game, he issued what was perhaps intended as a clarification. "I think everyone misinterpreted what I said . . . That wasn't what I said. It's what y'all interpreted it to be. I just asked the question . . . that's for you to answer. But that doesn't mean we don't like playing against it."

Huh? Say what? Casey Stengel could not have expressed it better.

Pre-game publicity, especially in Texas, had been deflected by two other events. On Tuesday, in the White House Bowl, Obama beat Romney, 51.1 to 47. And on Wednesday, in Austin, Darrell Royal died. Elections and death—none of that mattered on Saturday at Bryant-Denny Stadium, which looks down on the banks of the Black Warrior River. California wildfires do not generate as much smoke as the tailgate scene at Tuscaloosa, a parking lot metropolis, a crimson-clad population that's absolutely giddy on overdoses of Budweiser, Crown Royal, and Kraft yellow mustard. *Roll Tide!*

When Johnny Manziel conducted the orchestra to a 20–0 lead, the Roll Tide faction seemed mildly irritated and perhaps impatient, but largely unworried and certainly not panicky. McCarron would find a way.

Late in the fourth, sure enough, the crowd howled as McCarron and the Tide began to roll. A fifty-plus-yard pass completion put the ball inside the Aggies' ten-yard line. Then the Aggies held for three plays and a fourth-down life-or-death pass by McCarron was intercepted by Deshazor Everett. The Aggies had done it. They had defeated the undefeatable Crimson Tide and registered the biggest win in the entire hundred–plus years of Texas A&M football. The Aggie post-game locker room was not one of wild whoops and Gatorade baths. In fact, the mood was almost solemn, as the team realized it had accomplished something remarkable, something memorable. Sean Porter reflected on the fourth-down play. "Here was the deal," he remarked. "Do we stop them, or do we get scored on, like always?"

"It was eerie," said a visiting Aggie, describing the stadium scene in Alabama. "It was like, way off in the distance, you could hear Joan Baez singing 'The Night They Drove Old Dixie Down.'" What were discernible were the elevated voices of the Twelfth Man loyalists who were in the stands, outnumbered a thousand to one. They were yelling, "Heisman! Heisman!"

The final two regular-season games at College Station amounted to go-through-the-motions blowouts against Sam Houston State and Missouri. In the first game, a 47–28 rout, Johnny Manziel threw for 267 yards and three touchdowns, one of them on an eighty-nine-yard pass to Uzoma Nwachukwu on the Aggies' first offensive play of the second half. He added one hundred yards rushing with two TDs. The game put Manziel over three thousand yards passing and a thousand yards rushing for the season.

The Missouri game was just as one-sided, as Manziel passed for 372 yards and three touchdowns, adding two more TDs on the ground. The Aggies won by a score of 59–29 and raised their record to 10–2, giving them their first season with double-digit wins since 1998.

In the post-Alabama euphoria, those last two home victories were fun, but essentially anticlimactic. The moment that really mattered happened at the Heisman Trophy presentation at the

Marriot Marquis in New York City: Johnny Football became the first freshman ever to claim the most respected award in all of sports.

He won it, remarkably, as a product of the great unknown. College athletic departments devote more PR and marketing to their Heisman candidates Apple does before rolling out the Next Big Thing. Even by mid-October, hardly anybody outside of College Station had ever heard of Johnny Manziel. He took the thing in a landslide, over Notre Dame's Manti Te'o and the third-place vote-getter, Collin Klein, the quarterback from Kansas State. The voters had all seen the Alabama game. The Heisman electorate might be regionally prejudiced, and some of them might be dumb, but they're not *blind*.

With the Heisman comes football immortality. Jim Brown. Joe Namath. John Elway. Joe Montana. Peyton Manning. Those are names of some players who *didn't* win it. The beauty of the prize is that for every Earl Campbell and Tony Dorsett who *did* win, there are players like John Huarte and Eric Couch who played the game for nothing more than three hots and a cot and a college degree, but for one shining season did themselves and their schools proud.

The Aggies watched when Johnny Manziel accepted the award and made a speech, televised to the nation. It was evident that Manziel had written it himself, because the text was simple, sincere, and genuine— void of forced eloquence and buzz phrases that habitually spring from minds of professional ghostwriters. Johnny's speech went like this:

> This is a moment that I've dreamed about since I've been a kid, running around the backyard pretending I was Doug Flutie, throwing a Hail Mary to my dad. Now I'm so blessed to be on the stage with such a group of great guys and to be invited into this fraternity—what a pleasure it really is.
>
> I'd like to start by thanking the Heisman Trust and everybody that made this weekend possible. What a great experience it was to meet the people that I have—Manti, Collin—not only great football players, but great guys off the field as well. It's been a pleasure to get to know you guys better and I wish you all the best of luck.

Such an honor to represent Texas A&M and my teammates here tonight. I wish they could be on the stage with me. Texas A&M, choosing that school is one of the best decisions I've ever made in my entire life and I'm so proud to be a part of that.

To Mom, Dad, Mary, and the entire family watching—you mean the world to me. I just want to thank you for the encouragement, the love, and the patience over the years.

Grandpa, to all the times we used to play in the hallway and throw the ball until we couldn't anymore, I love you with all my heart and you inspired me to play football. Grandma, I'm so sorry for all the things we broke in the house.

To my coaches back at Kerrville Tivy—Mark Smith, Julius Scott, and everybody there—you taught us all what it meant to really fight and work for something that you wanted more than anything in the world. You taught us about passion and about heart and what it truly means to say, "Tivy fight never dies."

To Coach Sherman, Coach Rossley, Coach Sumlin, Coach Kingsbury, and everybody that's been a part of me playing football for my entire life, you've been truly a blessing. You taught me not only what it is to be a football player, but to be a man as well. For that, I thank you so much.

I wish my whole team can be up here with me tonight, especially my great offensive line and the whole offense. Luke Joeckel, Jarvis Harrison, Cedric Ogbuehi, Jake Matthews, and Patrick Lewis—I'm as safe standing here as I am in the pocket with you guys. You've done a great job of keeping me off my back and I can't thank you enough for everything. To all my teammates back home, I love you with all my heart.

I especially at this time would like to honor somebody who is near and dear to everybody at Texas A&M: Joey Villavisencio. Around this time last year, a center on our team passed away in a tragic car accident. It was something that as a whole team that we really had to fight through and press on through the bowl game. To Mr. and Mrs. Villavisencio, if I had a son, I would want him to be exactly like him. I know Joey is in a better place.

Most of all I want to thank God for allowing me to be here. All that he's blessed me with my entire life I'm so thankful for. For the love and the grace your have shown me, I'll be forever grateful.

The values that I have learned from my parents and that have been carried over by Texas A&M—leadership, respect, and putting others first is what the Twelfth Man is all about. I believe the Twelfth Man is one of the greatest traditions in all of college football—forty thousand students standing not as fans but as members of the team.

To the Twelfth Man, Texas A&M, Kerrville, Texas, and Aggies everywhere—this Heisman Trophy is for you.

Gig 'em!

For a twenty-year-old American male, two years can pass in a heartbeat. Johnny Manziel had traveled a road that began as the quarterback of the Kerrville Antlers and culminated in television appearances with Jay Leno and David Letterman. But beneath the euphoria was the looming reality that the Aggies had one more assignment on their to-do list: an appointment against Oklahoma in the AT&T Cotton Bowl. There were ominous overtones. The Sooners, as always, were a nightmarish opponent. And the Cotton Bowl had a reputation as a place where Heisman winners go to die. Roger Staubach, Earl Campbell, Bo Jackson, Tim Brown—all Heisman winners whose teams fell in the Cotton Bowl, their dream seasons ending on a bitter note.

The Aggies wouldn't let that happen. If Alabama had been the main course in the Aggies' most memorable season, Oklahoma would be the dessert. Manziel was unstoppable all night. In a 41–13 rout, he set a Cotton Bowl record with 516 yards in total offense, with two rushing touchdowns and two more in the air. Manziel performed like something out of a video game. The Sooners' defensive coordinator spent the game wincing on the sideline, like a man trying to pass a kidney stone.

So 2013 beckoned seductively to the best college quarterback in the nation. For Manziel, the new year would lead into a wonderland of misadventure.

7

TROUBLE

About a decade ago, some late-night talk show host described one aspect of Americana brilliantly. He pointed out that you know for sure that the holiday season is over when you go to the shopping mall and notice that Santa's workshop has been taken over by H&R Block.

January is a drag. It's a terrible way to begin the new year. In the aftermath of the parties and joyful gift giving, the great fellowship, the great food, and the even greater drink comes a time of sudden starkness, a stretch of the calendar when absolutely nothing worthwhile occurs. No matter what T. S. Eliot says, January is the cruelest month, with its short days and dismal weather. It's unrewarding for sports fans, and especially fans of college sports in Texas. During the autumn, everything revolves tightly around the football weekend. It's a time of raw pagan ritual and full-force purging of the dark demons that rest in the heart of every human being. The great football coach Darrell Royal acknowledged that football per se is a meaningless activity, except for its very important capacity to enable "college kids to blow off some steam." And nobody, but nobody, contains more steam than a college kid.

Come the end of the football season, and then the holiday stretch, after the last drink has been drunk and the last "Auld Lang Syne" has been sung, there comes a letdown of immeasurable proportions. It's a time of boredom and emptiness.

In other parts of the world, college students can occupy themselves with basketball. Not so, however, in Texas. Oh, colleges do have basketball teams and some of them are pretty good, and can play with anybody . . . sometimes. But nobody gives a damn about college basketball in Texas. Eavesdrop on any conversation, anytime, anywhere in Texas, and you will hear people discussing the advantages of socialism before basketball comes up. Texas wouldn't know a zone defense from a three-peckered goat.

The aforementioned Texas High School Football Coaches Association, in decades past, contributed to that situation. They made certain that basketball was swept under the carpet. During the basketball offseason, gyms were padlocked. Any kid who attended a summer basketball camp was deemed ineligible for competition. The football coaches' reasoning was simple: good, wholesome, athletic teenage boys needed to concentrate on football year-round. Live it, breathe it, eat it, drink it. Jones Ramsey, a sports publicist at Texas A&M during the Bear Bryant era, expressed it best: "There are two sports in Texas—football and football spring training."

That was a funny remark, but it was also all too true.

High school basketball players in Texas were cut from the same mold. Tall, yes, but also characterized by thick glasses, bad skin, and an overall unhealthy appearance that suggested malnutrition. They all carried asthma inhalers. That was pretty much the case at the colleges as well, and nowhere was that situation more pronounced than at Texas A&M. The Aggies played their home games at the G. Rollie White Coliseum, which was nothing more than a barn equipped with bleacher seats. The school eventually constructed a more state-of-the-art arena and even hired a top coach in the mid-1990s, a Texan with the all-Texas name of Billy Clyde Gillespie. Billy Clyde constructed a team that was good enough to reach the Sweet Sixteen, but when the Kentucky Wildcats offered him a job, he packed and bought a house in Lexington even before anybody in College Station realized that he was gone. Once at Kentucky, Gillespie learned to his dismay that the people in Kentucky not only cared about the sport, but they knew more about it than he did. They didn't like his style, and after one season, they ran him out of the state.

So, in January 2013, the mood around the Texas A&M campus was, as usual, in the wintertime doldrums. The natural high of the previous football season and the unprecedented performance of Johnny Manziel had been replaced by the natural letdown.

No one, it seemed, was more bored and restless than Johnny Manziel himself. Consider his situation and his plight. Hardly anyone since Charles Augustus Lindbergh had pole-vaulted from absolute obscurity into fame and recognition more quickly than Johnny Manziel had.

No, when it came to instant fame, Manziel was a one-of-a-kind specimen. And guess what? This was a kid who liked to have a good time. Blend that factor in with the reality that Manziel was a gifted-at-birth media magnet and it did not require Sherlock Holmes to deduce that Johnny Football was about to become a combustible commodity.

Somewhere in the backrooms of Big Media, the news purveyors had been rubbing their hands together and muttering, "We can make this kid into something bigger than he really is. If he doesn't have the true qualities for controversy, then we'll give him some."

The first inklings of what was to come happened in New York in December 2012, the night of the Heisman presentation. A photo of Manziel dining with his family was circulated. Manziel's entourage was drinking champagne and Johnny Football was nursing a soda pop. The message that came with the photograph was an implied innuendo that said, "Yeah, he's sippin' that Diet Dr. Pepper, but you can be sure that he's got a flagon of bubbly hidden under the table. And you realize, of course, that he's underage."

Soon, more photographs of Johnny at play appeared. Here was Johnny courtside at a Dallas Mavericks game against the Miami Heat. The TV cameras focused on the Aggie, and the on-the-air announcers wondered, "How does a college kid afford that ticket? Who paid for that?" It was at this point, mid-January, that this author was thinking, "Watch it, Johnny. They're coming after you."

Used to be, the sports media went to extreme lengths to protect the image of its superstars. Take Babe Ruth. This was a guy who, on the night after a game and the night before another one, would rent a suite at the Book Cadillac Hotel in Detroit, invite half the city to come on up, stand on a chair, and announce, "Any woman in here who doesn't want to fuck can leave right now." A New York newspaper columnist was present at such a gathering but never reported it. The Babe had a huge and insatiable hunger for rich food and young women. He would routinely visit the most expensive restaurant in town, scan the menu, and say to the waiter, "Hi, pal. I believe I'll have the breast of young teenager."

None of this ever made it into public print until long after Babe was dead. But the example of Babe Ruth serves as a classic example, Exhibit A, as to how the American sportswriter has been transformed from protector/enabler into the snitch.

So every media outlet—be it print, broadcast TV, or online—and every blog was waiting there conspicuously in Johnny's shadow, poised and waiting and eager to pounce. The marquee name "Johnny Football" translated into "celebrity." Like Justin Bieber. Therefore Johnny Football had become a marked man. The message was plain: "He's gonna screw up. Just you wait. You'll see."

Manziel, at first, seemed oblivious to the media menace and then, perhaps out of a sense of naïve youth, proceeded to tempt fate. It was January, still, and someone posted an iPhone photo of Manziel at the WinStar World Casino in Oklahoma, displaying a fistful of C-notes.

"Holy shit!" cried the media.

"So what?" Manziel countered, via Twitter. He pointed out that he was in an eighteen-and-over facility and there was nothing illegal about winning a pot full of dough. A day or so later, Johnny appeared at yet another NBA courtside, this time in Houston at a Rockets-Clippers game, where he met Clippers star Chris Paul. Later he collaborated with a trick-shot specialty group that calls itself Dude Perfect to create a video. And it was still January.

Come February, Johnny was sighted (where else?) at New Orleans at Mardi Gras and photographed with Justin Timberlake and Jessica Biel. And then, Johnny, for some reason, materialized way the hell off in Toronto attending a concert by Canadian recording star Drake. Manziel called that the highlight of his offseason. Perhaps Johnny Football, at this point, should have taken heed of a quote from Drake himself that appeared in a profile about him in *Rolling Stone*: "The press is evil."

So how did Johnny Manziel maintain his class load at College Station while jet-setting around like the guy in Carly Simon's hit song "You're So Vain"? Easy. He was taking four courses online, advancing steadily toward the attainment of his degree in sports management. If he behaved himself, and studied hard, he might grow up to be a sports management personality of the stature of Jerry Jones or Cincinnati's Marge Schott. Manziel pointed out, and accurately, that he could not make it regularly to classroom lectures on time because everywhere he went on campus, he was mobbed by students wanting to be in photos with him.

Spring football practice served as a respite from the rip-roaring offseason. Manziel made some headlines in one practice for shoving a graduate assistant in frustration after throwing an interception. In the Aggies spring game that drew over seventy-thousand fans and was televised nationally on ESPN, he made waves again for crashing into a linebacker head-on while throwing a block. Kevin Sumlin, while praising the kid's spunk, publicly chastised, or at least voiced concerns over, his star's apparent lack of awareness when it came to the concept of self-endangerment. What Sumlin was essentially saying was, "If Johnny goes out and breaks his neck, he might as well break mine along with it."

Johnny Football's response, while not in so many words, was basically, "Sure, Coach. Whatever you say. But I don't have time for that discussion right now because I've got to head down to the beach scene at Cabo San Lucas. Spring break! Party time! Chiquitas and ceviche! Adios!"

Certain Texas A&M football purists might have been perplexed when another photo of Manziel appeared, this time with Johnny sporting a spray-on tattoo that was the orange logo of the Texas Longhorns on one of his biceps. In Aggieland theology, that was tantamount to a swastika. But any dismay over that was dispelled by a great picture of Johnny getting kissed on both sides of his face by two half-naked beach bunnies. People were beginning to get the impression that life as Johnny Football was not all that bad and that Johnny Football was figuring that out as well. And, understanding the pressures of life that comes with the spotlight, during the peak of NCAA March Madness, he tweeted his support for controversial Ole Miss basketball star Marshall Henderson who, among other questionable activities, had been busted buying $800 worth of marijuana with counterfeit currency.

April came, and Johnny Manziel threw out the first ball at the Texas Rangers home opener against the Los Angeles Angels of Anaheim. Ex-Ranger idol Josh Hamilton, by then in an Angels' uniform, got practically booed out of the ball park. That partially had to do with a quote from Hamilton in which he said that Dallas was a football town, not a baseball town. Well, he had a point. The guy throwing out the first ball was not, after all, a player on the Texas A&M baseball team. The cascade of cheers for Johnny Football could be heard practically to Waco.

Then, it was back to his old home town, Kerrville, where he attended a charity golf event and was photographed in a car holding a joint. Johnny explained that the image was digitally altered.

Anyway, who cared? He was off to the Big Apple, not to receive the Heisman Trophy this time, but to attend a Yankees game and UFC 159 on the same day.

Then, to offset the stresses of completing those online courses at A&M, Johnny traveled to San Diego, where he reenacted a scramble-fumble-TD pass play that he pulled off in the Alabama game. That happened on the field of a Padres game before he threw out the first ball. Afterward, it was on to a round of golf at Pebble Beach, where Johnny Football shot 79. And then he appeared in a music video with country star Granger Smith.

In a trial in Fort Worth, a sixteen-year-old rich kid who had killed four people in a drunken wreck was the "victim," his attorney argued, of a condition that was termed "affluenza." Johnny's family was reported to have been well-to-do. Johnny Football drove a gently used Mercedes. Around the nation certain sports columnists, guys with swollen prostates and bad marriages, began to complain about the Heisman Trophy winner's flamboyant, if not out-and-out hedonist lifestyle. Manziel was bemused, and tweeted, with honesty and justification, "I'm twenty years old. I'm not hurting anyone." Except, perhaps, himself.

School was out. Johnny passed his online courses and headed to Miami to attend the NBA finals—a dandy, Heat versus Spurs— and had a photo taken with LeBron James. He and LeBron were becoming fast friends.

So the Johnny Manziel world tour would scarcely miss a beat, while the dark forces of the media continued to lie in ambush, waiting for some morsels of red meat. And, rather predictably, Johnny Football finally did something to feed the beast.

Back for a breather in College Station, perhaps recuperating from an exhausting social agenda, Johnny Football became upset after a getting a parking ticket from a campus cop. He tweeted, for the benefit of his 368,000 followers, the following: "Shit like tonight is the reason why I can't wait to leave College Station, whenever it might be."

Well, the feces finally hit the fan, with a big-time splat.

Johnny, perhaps guilty of TWI (tweeting while impaired), retreated and retracted as quickly as he could: "Don't ever forget that I love A&M with all my heart, but please, please walk a mile in my shoes." But once a tweet gets out of the bag, there is no possible way to get it back inside.

Johnny Football's universal fan base—at least the portion that wore maroon attire and would drink three bottles a day of maroon wine if such a product existed—was devastated. Right away, a staffer for the Texas A&M newspaper, the *Battalion*, fired off a campus first: an anti–Johnny Manziel manifesto. The staffer, Sean Lester, produced an op-ed column under the daunting headline "Johnny Be Gone." It read, in part:

> Texas A&M quarterback Johnny Manziel is, once again, at the center of the sports world's attention. There's little sympathy and fewer people on his side. Johnny Football has made an uncalculated mistake that will have ramifications. It's time to send Johnny Football down the proverbial one-year hallway in the house that is Texas A&M and straight out the door.
>
> A day in Manziel's shoes would equal a lifetime for many of us "regular people." His accomplishments are noted. But no matter the outcome of a promising 2013 season, it is time to watch Manziel ride off into the sunset.
>
> Johnny Football wants out, and as a selfish observer, I want him out too. The football program is more relevant now than it has been at any point in more than one hundred years of activity. But more importantly, I want to see how Kevin Sumlin and the other 100 players on the roster prove that it isn't just the Johnny Manziel show and that A&M, as a program, can contend for years.

That took some guts on the part of Sean Lester, who was also a defenseman on Texas A&M's ice hockey team. Johnny Manziel offered no response, hoping that his apologetic retraction would enable, with time, the whole mess to be forgotten. Too late, of course. That infamous little nineteen-word tweet would resonate nationally, serve as the lead story on ESPN *SportsCenter*, and land atop the front page of Yahoo! and countless other major outlets. (Somewhere in the great beyond, Babe Ruth was thanking providence for the fact that he never had a Twitter account.)

Johnny Football had committed his first major screw-up, and from that point forward, any of Johnny's social ventures would be tainted in a sinister context by media ghouls who masqueraded as the Knights of the First Amendment. Johnny didn't let them down. During midsummer, Manziel materialized far behind enemy lines. He showed up uninvited at a fraternity party (translate that into "beer bust") on the University of Texas campus. Were that not outlandish enough, he chose to wear a Tim Tebow football jersey for the occasion. God. What a contrast. Tebow, the heaven-bound Bible banger. Manziel, the hell-raiser.

The habitually addled UT frat boys (the author ought to know, as he used to be one) asked Manziel to leave and he was escorted off the property. By this point, it was becoming plain to amateur behavioral analysts that Johnny Manziel had evolved from a spontaneous free spirit into a character who was gaining large measures of amusement by fucking with people's minds.

August was approaching and with it came more tawdry publicity. Johnny Manziel had been one of a handful of top college quarterbacks invited to appear as guest instructors at the Manning Passing Academy. That's a football camp conducted on the campus of Nicholls State University at Thibodaux, Louisiana, and operated under the aegis of ex–New Orleans Saints quarterback idol Archie Manning and his two sons, Peyton and Eli. Among former campers is Russell Wilson. Kids at the camp get tutored by the top names in the game. It isn't cheap—the camping experience costs $585 a day, although enrollees each receive a free football worth $100.

Word would quickly circulate that Manziel had arrived and, after an undisclosed period, been asked to leave on the authority of

Archie Manning himself. Manziel had been a no-show at a morning staff meeting. The talk on the football street had it that Manziel had been too hungover to greet the day.

Johnny denied that. He said that he had merely overslept and his alarm malfunctioned because his cell phone was dead. He did concede to have been socializing that evening before with a girl he had met in a bar. Harmless enough. You can't put a man in jail for getting lucky, but Johnny Football had once again been tried and convicted in the media courtroom—and an ocean of bad ink was the result.

At a midsummer SEC preseason football media powwow, Johnny and his coach, Sumlin, represented the Aggies. The press event happened in the immediate wake of the football camp brouhaha and thus was ill-timed for Johnny's purposes. Naturally, the topic was what had happened at Manziel's Q and A session. He reiterated his innocence. "I overslept. There is nothing more to talk about. The rumors about other stuff weren't really true." Media people took careful note of the word "really" and the beat went on, along with Johnny Football's turbulent offseason.

He flew to L.A. to attend the ESPY Awards as the Best Male College Athlete of 2012 and then flew to Bryan, Texas, where he would enter a guilty plea to the charge of failure to identify from the tavern event that preceded his freshman on-the-field season. A variety of other charges, such as disorderly conduct, were dropped.

By then, Manziel had become much better recognized as a nocturnal wayfarer than a Heisman Trophy–winning marvel, and it seemed that the clichéd identity of a walking time bomb had been created especially for him. Even the famed on-air shrink Dr. Phil (McGraw), himself a native Texan, issued some pithy thoughts on the Manziel craziness. In an interview with the CBS affiliate in Dallas, her said:

> Let's think about it. You're twenty years old and a mega star. You've got hero worship and adulation. I live in Los Angeles and see actors

out there young and old who get a real God complex because they start to believe all of the hype. It knocks you off balance and you start making bad decisions. "I'm a star and I'm supposed to show up late," and people get upset with you and all of a sudden it's like, "Wait a minute. I'm supposed to be the Golden Boy here." So you lash out. Is it shocking to see that from someone with that level of maturity? Not really.

I was fifty years old and went to Hollywood and launched the *Dr. Phil Show*. By then, if you don't really know who you are, you probably aren't going to figure it out. I've got a wife who will take me by the ear and say, "You've got to calm down." Here's the problem. I see it all the time in Hollywood. You get surrounded by people who tell you what you don't want to hear and you replace them with a bunch of sycophants. Trust me. Every pro team is watching this behavior, and you damage your chances.

Johnny Football could have absorbed Dr. Phil's warning, if that was what he had intended, and rightfully responded that yeah, he gets it, but it's a little too late in the offseason to go out and collect a whole bunch of new friends. But maybe the champagne was beginning to turn to vinegar and the alternative universe of instant celebrity-hood was not all that it had seemed to be at first. Manziel's parents—whom Dr. Phil had actually praised: "They obviously gave him a sound work ethic. How could they have foreseen all this sudden onslaught of fame and notoriety?"—appeared on an *Outside the Lines* episode on ESPN. They revealed that their son had undergone anger management and alkie counseling, a positive thing that the media quickly spun into a negative. Johnny's father did suggest that in his son's pressure cooker world, a big time meltdown could occur.

The troubled offseason of Johnny Football was about to come to an end with the opening of fall practice in College Station, and for Manziel, it could not come quickly enough. The echo of the drum beat of negativity, the tut-tuts and tsk-tsks, resounded from all corners. "Great athletes know that in order to become a champion, you have to play and you have to REST hard," was the declaration of some asshole.

So when Manziel arrived with his teammates for the beginning of two-a-day workouts and the launching of the Aggies' quest for a national championship, he'd been transposed from Johnny Football into Al Capone. Well, Manziel thought that from there on, now that football was back in earnest, he could let his quarterbacking prowess do all of the talking. He was featured on the cover of *Texas Monthly* magazine in an artsy Superman pose. All seemed okay again in the Aggie universe of Johnny Football.

Then, one day during practice, ESPN reported that way back in the previous January, Manziel had sat in a New Haven, Connecticut, hotel room, signed approximately three hundred items of memorabilia that were arranged on a king-sized bed, and received a flat fee of five figures from an autograph broker. If those allegations were substantiated, the NCAA might well suspend Manziel for the entire season.

Johnny Football before the game against Sam Houston State at Kyle Field, September 2013. *AP Images.*

Kyle Field at Texas A&M University. *Getty Images.*

The Twelfth Man statue on the Texas A&M campus. *Getty Images.*

Texas A&M head coach Kevin Sumlin. *AP Images.*

Former Texas A&M offensive coordinator Kliff Kingsbury. *Getty Images.*

Manziel eludes pressure outside the pocket against SMU, September 15, 2012.
AP Images.

Manziel runs around the tackle of Sam Houston State's defender Robert Shaw for a touchdown, November 17, 2012. *AP Images.*

Aggies receiver Uzoma Nwachukwu catches a pass for a first down against Oklahoma in the AT&T Cotton Bowl Classic, January 4, 2013. *AP Images.*

Manziel finds running room against the Oklahoma Sooners in the Cotton Bowl, January 4, 2013. *AP Images.*

Johnny Manziel at the Heisman Award ceremonies, December 8, 2012. *Getty Images.*

Gig 'em! Manziel speaks to the press after winning the Heisman, December 8, 2012. *AP Images.*

Aggies wide receiver Mike Evans awaits the start of the game against Sam Houston State, September 7, 2013. *AP Images.*

Manziel is tackled by Auburn defenders LaDarius Owens (10) and Ryan White (18), October 11, 2013. *AP Images.*

Manziel carries the ball against Duke in the Chick-fil-A Bowl, December 31, 2013. *AP Images.*

8

OIL IN THE FAMILY

BACK DURING THE EARLY MONTHS of 2013, when this author was first exploring the notion of writing a book that chronicled the exploits of Johnny Football, a very casual acquaintance told him, "I have a distant relative who lives in Tyler who said that when Johnny was growing up there as a little boy, none of the kids in his neighborhood were allowed to play with him because his family were gangsters."

The author—who's had worse things actually said about him— dismissed that as yet another incidence of what might be termed the collateral damage that is incurred by those who attain the rank of overnight celebrity.

People say the damnedest things.

However, deep into the summer of Johnny Manziel's discontent, an article appeared that shed light upon the football star's very interesting, even fascinating, family lineage. The article appeared not in investigative outlets like the *New York Times* or *Washington Post*, but rather on the sports gossip website *Deadspin*, which uses the F-word frequently in its headlines.

Mainstream media have been known to categorize *Deadspin* as the "*National Inquirer* of sports" without somehow realizing that the *National Inquirer* is frequently spot-on with its stories and produces more genuine journalistic scoops than all the mainstream media outlets combined. Thus the same could be said of *Deadspin*. Its revelations on the Manziel clan eclipsed by far any of the previous publicity concerning the life and times of Johnny Football.

The saga began in 1883 with the birth of Johnny Football's great-great-grandfather, Joseph Manziel, in the Lebanon Mountain region of Syria. That, in itself, was a bit of an eye-opener. Most Texans had assumed due to his appearance that Manziel, like Dallas Cowboys quarterback Tony Romo, was part Hispanic. Manziel and Romo somewhat resembled one another.

Joe Manziel and his wife would immigrate to the United States, bringing with them their two-year-old son, Esahiah. They settled in Louisiana and began pursuing the American Dream with the zeal of a greyhound chasing an electric rabbit.

Joseph Manziel's business activities involved mineral exploration and his career, like those of his eventual offspring, can be traced through the stern and irrefutable sanctity of courthouse records—county, state, and federal. So that paper trail got started in 1921, with a lawsuit that heavily involved a business transaction dealing with Manziel. The details of the case were complex, but hardly unusual in the oil business then or now. The fundamentals entailed a dispute that involved allegations of a back-dated lease and a lawyer of questionable ethics.

That ended in 1923 when a justice of the Louisiana supreme court, in a written opinion, found that Joseph Manziel had presented "a highly unlikely story," and the justice went on to state that he was "fully convinced that Manziel was part of a crooked and dishonest transaction and he was, in fact, a party to it."

Thus a tall and sturdy family tree took root. Joseph was the patriarch, but legacy hit its stride fulltime with activities of the son, Esahiah, who decided that in Louisiana, he might advance his cause more expeditiously if he ditched his given name and operated instead as Bobby Joe Manziel. Bobby Joe, like his great-grandson Johnny Football, was a skilled athlete. He boxed professionally, using the stage name "the Syrian Kid," and became a sparring partner of a better known pugilist named Jack Dempsey. Dempsey was second only perhaps to Babe Ruth in fame and glory during the 1920s in what was reflectively known as the Golden Era of American sports.

Bobby Joe Manziel, upon the decline of his prizefighting skills, became a fight promoter and a writer, two occupations that are rightfully associated with difficulty and heartache. Bobby Joe encountered his right at the start. At a time when professional wrestling operated under the guise of a legitimate competition, Bobby Joe was accused of fixing a heavyweight match between the Greek champion, Jim Londos, and a Russian contestant named Count Ivan Zarynoff.

The allegations proved legitimate enough for the state of Louisiana to yank Bobby Joe's license. In desperation, Bobby Joe hightailed it across the state line into East Texas with two bucks in his pocket. In the process, he ditched his wife and infant daughter. The wife obtained a divorce, but the daughter, named Gloria, would show up listed as an heir in various lawsuits that happened throughout the procession of passing years.

At some point, Bobby Joe developed a passion for the pursuit of underground riches—fossil fuels—and became convinced that he had a God-given talent for discovering the treasure that lay beneath the piney woods of East Texas. There was plenty of it down there, that was for sure. Bobby Joe's platform for riches took shape for good when he became convinced a substantial pool of oil was ready for harvest within the subsurface of the property of the Negro New Hope Baptist Church.

Manziel required two things to go after it. First, he needed to secure the permission of the parishioners, and secondly, he needed the money to drill. He approached the second task first. He telegraphed his old sparring partner, Jack Dempsey, with the news of an investment opportunity. The Manassa Mauler, as he was known, would, in his autobiography, contend that he scarcely remembered Bobby Joe and what recollections he did have were that of Manziel as his chauffeur and not as a former sparring partner.

But, thought Dempsey, what the hell? It's only money. He wired $400 to Bobby Joe Manziel. Then, one by one, Manziel went to work on the church people. He started with the deacons and then, according to a newspaper account, "chased down the remaining Negro church goers in his flivver until all forty agreed to provide permission to drill in the church's back yard."

Soon, Jack Dempsey was pleased to receive a 1,000 percent return on his original $400 investment, and thus, to paraphrase the final line from the motion picture *Casablanca*, was the beginning of a beautiful friendship. Dempsey agreed to back Manziel in dozens of drilling ventures. The first eleven, following the churchyard gusher, were dry holes, or in the vernacular of Texas oil hounds, "five-star dusters." But the losing streak could not and would not last forever, and Manziel soon became a lifetime member of the American Society of Petrosexuals. His wells supplied high-grade crude in such abundance that the Manziel-Dempsey partnership was soon facing allegations that the pair "openly and aggressively" ignored state and local limits on production.

The Texas attorney general dragged Manziel into court six times during an eight-month span on charges ranging from overproduction to operating illegal bypasses (slant-hole drilling), not storing oil for proper measurement, and failure to pay proper royalties. All Manziel was doing was following the basic guidelines for the Texas billionaires club, but he found himself doing some jail time for disobeying the state's injunction. (In other words, he probably bribed the wrong guy.)

Once back on the street, Bobby Joe and Jack faced new charges from the Texas Railroad Commission, which oversees all aspects of the state's drilling operations, including "chronic violations" of its various policies. But two weeks later, a judge gave the heave-ho to those charges and, for good measure, socked the Texas Rangers, who'd enforced the commission's allegations, with a contempt rap.

That was followed up by even more resounding courtroom triumph, which, until Johnny Football captured the Heisman trophy, was the biggest win in the Manziels' extended and storied family history.

In an East Texas U.S. district court, Manziel brought a suit that contended the federal government's regulatory capacities must be limited to interstate commerce and the fed's arm of authority did not extend to him, since he only did business in Texas. The court ruled in favor of Bobby Joe in a decision that would, according to *Time* magazine, affect the oil industry "for good."

An assistant U.S. attorney, Charles I. Francis, told the magazine that "as far as the federal government is concerned, oil regulation is wrecked." That never kept Bobby Joe out the state courts to defend various complaints that included fraud, deceit, malicious contrivance, and attempting to drill for oil in an unfenced area frequented by school children. He was in the big time.

Prosperity embraced the active world of Bobby Joe Manziel, and in 1937, he married an eighteen-year-old LSU student, Dorothy Nolan, whom he had met "a few years earlier at a Syrian convention." Oil patch profits also enabled him to plunge full-throttle into yet another passion—cockfighting. That area of sporting competition had been illegal in Texas since before the time Joe Manziel immigrated from Syria, but the pastime would flourish in the backwoods, and Bobby Joe would note that that at one point there were more illicit cockfighting pits in East Texas than movie theaters. He owned a stable of at least 1,200 "battle roosters," and one prized breed of game fowl, the Manziel grey, is of course named in his honor.

One big setback occurred in 1950, when he turned the ignition key of his new cabin cruiser and the boat blew up. It was never determined whether the source of the explosion was an assassination attempt. Manziel was hospitalized for weeks, but he rebounded in grand style.

Bobby Joe liked life on the center stage, and he liked public spectacles, so he enticed Dempsey to join him in the construction of an indoor arena in Tyler that would offer a seating capacity larger than Madison Square Garden's. The building that he called the Oil Palace would hold twenty thousand spectators, and the persons up front would watch activities from what had been the box seats at the 1956 Democratic National Convention in Chicago.

But Bobby Joe died in 1956, and his plans for the grandiose Oil Palace died along with him. The box seats from the political convention were given, or sold, to a church. Later, a more modest Oil Palace with seven thousand seats—more appropriate for the city the size of Tyler—would be built.

His son, Bobby Joe the younger, maintained family traditions. His business activities were nicely summarized in a ruling issued by Irving Goldberg, a justice with the U.S. Fifth Circuit Court of Appeals in New Orleans. Justice Goldberg wrote:

In 1963, Howard Wallace Barbee and Bobby Joe Manziel, then gullible and motivated by avarice, lost $10,000 in a confidence racket. The memory of that hoax lingered with them and two years later, still motivated by avarice, sought to recoup their losses by instigating the same racket for their benefit. The only difference was that the intended victim notified police and Barbee and Manziel were arrested and convicted in federal district court of possession altered currency. Their appeal, unlike many of the criminal cases that come before us, is not burdened with significant factual disputations. Barbee and Manziel admit the facts of their scheme and concede that it may have been morally reprehensible. They contest merely its illegality.

The confidence racket which was employed in 1963 and in 1965 involves a "stir man," a genuine federal reserve note, an altered federal reserve note, and of course a "sucker." The "stir man" contacts a "sucker" and shows him a "counterfeit" reserve note which is an exact duplicate of a genuine note and which even experts would claim to be genuine. He guarantees that a revolutionary duplication process can be put in motion for quite a reasonable investment. To the "sucker's" dismay, after contributing his share of the investment, he learns that both reserve notes were genuine and that the only process performed had been the altering of serial numbers and other markings on one note to correspond with the other.

What a delightful and, at the same time, brilliant legal argument. Sadly for Manziel, the federal appeals court declined to buy it.

Bobby Joe the younger eventually got in trouble with the law. In 1980, he was indicted for conspiracy charges involving the murder of a Tyler grocer over gambling debts. Manziel hired a high-profile prosecutor from the DA's office in Dallas, Doug Mulder, to switch over to the defense side on his behalf. Mulder had been one of the real-life stars in the famed documentary *The Thin Blue Line*, in which he railroaded an innocent man, Randall Dale Adams, who was eventually exonerated, for the murder of a Dallas cop.

Mulder got Manziel good results; the charges were dropped. Still, Bobby Joe had one last scrape with fuzz left in him. In 2002 he was indicted on charges connected with cocaine but served a brief sentence after a plea bargain arrangement. His reputation in Tyler suffered, as evidenced in courtroom testimony from a police witness in a case involving a bank robbery in which Bobby Joe was not implicated:

COURT: Do you suspect Bobby Joe Manziel of being a participant in the activities of the Dixie Mafia?
WITNESS: Your honor, that's what I've heard on the street from other police officers.

As of the spring of 2014, Bobby Joe was operating the scaled-down Tyler Oil Palace, where he has greeted and welcomed the likes of Glenn Beck and Sarah Palin.

Bobby Joe's little brother, Norman "Big Paul" Manziel, is Johnny Football's grandfather. He is the same man praised so eloquently by Johnny in his Heisman speech, the man who taught him how to throw a football. Big Paul, in the early nineties, served seven months on a conviction of witness tampering in the aftermath of a DWI arrest—small change and a piddling accusation when compared to the exploits of his father and brother.

Then, in the final weeks of the summer of 2013, a fifth generation of Manziel—the incredible Johnny Football—would find himself in what amounted to the courtroom facing a serious charge, and his trial would receive more publicity than all of his forebears combined. That should have been easily predicted by genetic scientists. Let us take it back at least to the original Manziel, the Syrian immigrant Joe. He was the stud, and like Man o' War, and Citation and Secretariat and Seattle Slew, and down through the generations, the offspring, no matter the quality of the brood mare, shared one common trait. They all had pawn shop balls, and they weren't afraid of anything or anybody. And they didn't give a damn what anybody might have thought about their daily ethic, which was, "Be your own bad self." Old Joe Manziel might have passed along a kernel or two of advice to his great-great-grandson Johnny. There are a lot of impaired drivers on the road less traveled, and parenthetically, if you push the envelope long enough, you're gonna get licked.

Johnny Football's court was a different kind than was experienced by his less renowned ancestors. There would be no police witnesses, no FBI, and no hard-charging federal prosecutors. And if convicted, Johnny would face no jail time. Actually, his situation was even worse.

The accusers were the hard-eyed enforcement branch of the National Collegiate Athletic Association. The accusation—accepting money for signing autographs—constituted a serious breach of conduct for one of the organization's student athletes. Terrelle Pryor of Ohio State had been suspended for exchanging athletic merchandise not only for money, but also for complimentary tattoos. The resulting ramifications of that scandal got the Buckeyes slapped with big-time sanctions and cost the coach, Jim Tressel, his job.

The case against Manziel, according to ESPN reports, was this: An autograph broker told sources that on January 11 and 12, 2013, Johnny Football traveled to New Haven to attend a function held by the Walter Camp Football Foundation. While in town, the broker alleged, Manziel was paid $7,500 (not the five-figure amount that had originally been reported) to visit the room at the Omni Hotel and sign three hundred mini and full-sized football helmets. Unbeknownst to Manziel, the event was recorded on video, which the broker had taken to guarantee to buyers that the autographs were authentic.

At one point, the broker inquired if Manziel would accept additional money for personalizing some of the inscriptions. Manziel declined, saying that he had before, but that it had raised questions.

The case of the NCAA vs. Johnny Football looked bad for the player as presented in the media reports. But whether in a criminal courtroom or an NCAA investigation, something beyond circumstantial evidence would be required for the hammer to fall. Nowhere in the damning hotel-room video was Manziel actually recorded discussing a payoff amount, much less actually accepting any cash.

The rumors, the innuendo, the media flak. It all was raised to a stupendous crescendo. Many residents in the Aggie kingdom were convinced that the entire issue was a setup engineered by evil people in Alabama seeking vengeance for their defeat at the hands of Manziel and another one looming in College Station in September. Improbable? Sure, but everybody loves conspiracy theories.

One popular topic of barroom sports discussion involved Manziel's reputation for being the product of a family of significant financial means.

Question: Why would a rich kid like Johnny risk his entire career over a lousy $7,500?

Probable answer: A kid can buy a shitload of Bud Lite with a lousy $7,500.

If convicted—if that was the proper term—Manziel would likely serve a one-season suspension, and all of the hopes for the 2013 season would vanish, along with the serious pipeline of Aggie alum revenue that had been created by Johnny Mania. There was even speculation that Manziel might have to forfeit his Heisman award, like Reggie Bush at USC in the aftermath of slush-fund sanctions.

Another central character in his dreary soap opera was Nate Fitch, Manziel's old pal, former roommate, designated driver, and the go-to guy, according to the reports, when it came to organizing autograph sessions for Johnny Football. NCAA investigators would be grilling Nate Fitch as well, and if he said something dumb, then goodbye Johnny.

What a nightmare. As the hearsay-laden media dispatches increased in both number and fervor, the skies around College Station seemed to darken, and many of the cadet corps Aggies were shaking in their senior boots. The Texas A&M athletic department took the extreme measure of retaining the Birmingham, Alabama, law firm of Lightfoot, Franklin, and White to protect the interests of the school in this affair. That was same firm that had helped Auburn cover its ass during the sideshow of allegations that Cam Newton's father had sought payments from Mississippi State in return for delivering his superstar son to its doorstep.

Even Dez Bryant, the receiver for the Dallas Cowboys who maintained a highly polished knack for controversy of his own, decided to introduce his thoughts into the Manziel-NCAA-autograph discussion. Bryant may be the most attention-seeking player in the history of football. During the 2013 season, TV cameras showed him screaming at teammates at the height of a Category 5 temper eruption that Texas women refer to as a hissy-fit.

So from that ridiculous moment on, the geniuses who produce NFL telecasts decreed that the camera, when the Dallas offense was off the field, would focus entirely on close-ups of Dez Bryant, hoping to capture more of his staged histrionics. Bryant was fully aware that the cameras were closing in on him, and only him, and accommodated the networks with emotional displays worthy of the leading actor in a silent movie. Had Bryant been perhaps offering a little more attention to what was actually happening on the field, the Cowboys might not have missed the playoffs again.

Anyway, Dez decided, entirely uninvited, to mount the Manziel debate dais. He'd been suspended for his final season at Oklahoma State for lying to the NCAA about a lunch visit with a potential agent named Deion Sanders. It's always the cover-up that bites you on the ass, and never the actual crime. Dez Bryant should have entered politics, and who is to say that he someday won't? So Dez declared that if he received a one-year suspension, so should Johnny Football. The circumstances were entirely different, but that didn't keep Dez's mouth shut. "I'll be mad as hell if the NCAA doesn't suspend him for a year. I'll be mad," the pass-catcher said. Why anybody cared what Dez thought was a mystery of its own, but the brightest minds in sports media presented his rant with a front page-top story of the newscast forum.

Poor Manziel. He was stuck in the one-hundred-degree-heat-index hell of Texas football practices preparing for the season, unsure that there would even be a season for him. Coach Sumlin kept his quarterback quarantined from the media while limiting his own comments to terse "let's wait and see" half-sentences.

ESPN.com did manage to provide some meaningful quotes from an unnamed former NCAA investigator. Usually in media coverage, "unnamed source" translates into somebody the reporter made up, but if this source was indeed fictional, he still made sense.

"In order to penalize Manziel, the NCAA is going to have to provide proof that he received the autograph payments," the source said. "If Manziel and Fitch stick to their stories, and the autograph brokers remain silent, then the NCAA is going to have a hard time proving it."

Finally D-Day arrived. The hearing, of course, would be sealed off from public and media scrutiny. Still, it was the greatest event of its kind since the Scopes monkey trial in the 1920s. Manziel, who had a lawyer that his family had retained, sat behind closed doors inside the Texas A&M athletic offices and answered questions from NCAA investigators. The hearing took six hours, and for Manziel, it was a day that must have seemed longer than a whore's dream.

What loomed next was the elegant torture of awaiting the NCAA's determination of the issue. That could take weeks. It certainly had done so in previous cases. It was as if the high priests of college athletics ethics took fiendish delight in placing their "persons of interest" on a rotisserie and letting the poor saps turn ever so slowly over the hot coals of righteousness.

Now Kevin Sumlin and the Texas A&M athletic staff found itself waist-deep in a Catch-22 proposition. Should they put Manziel on the field while the NCAA made up its mind? The school itself could face sanctions. *Sports Illustrated* noted that in practice, Manziel was taking most of the snaps with the first team and accurately read the tea leaves. "If the Aggies are concerned that the NCAA will pull Manziel off the field, they aren't acting like it," the magazine reported. "The coaching staff . . . is going ahead as if Manziel will start Saturday [against Rice] and beyond."

The president of the college, John Sharp, a career Texas politician who gave up running for statewide office a decade before because he was a Democrat, issued words of assurance for the Aggie faithful. He declared that he knew, and knew for certain, that the NCAA would let Manziel off the hook. The Aggie faithful wondered how John Sharp knew that and remained skeptical. "If John Sharp is so damn smart, then why isn't he a Republican?"

Four days after the hearing, the NCAA delivered two bombshells. The first was that it had reached a decision, a verdict of sorts, in four days. Only four days. And the ruling was that while Manziel had inadvertently violated a rule or two, there was no courtroom-worthy evidence that he had taken a nickel. The punishment:

Johnny Manziel would be suspended for the season opener against the Rice Owls at College Station. But, seeing as how all of those people had bought tickets and would be driving in from all over the state to see Johnny Football, they only suspended him for the first half. End of investigation.

Around the football nation, fans and commentators were popping gut strings over what the majority seemed to feel was a shamefully modest sentence. "A half slap on the wrist," they called it.

The concept of "self-righteous" might have been called into question, but there was no doubt about the volume of indignation. Muffled sobs could be heard in editorial offices throughout the land. Up the highway in Waco, home of a city full of Aggie-hating Baptists, the student newspaper called the Baylor *Lariat* expressed dismay that was typical: "Johnny Manziel is no stranger to preferential treatment," the paper declared. "Behind Manziel's fame and fortune is the story of a kid who has a lot of growing up to do, while the NCAA allows him to sink. . . . The suspension of 'Johnny Football' exposes the NCAA and BCS for the mismanaged and corrupt organization that it is."

Even the Aggie students, well, some of them, expressed surprise. But one student, Jonah Eddleman, was certain of one thing: "When Manziel runs out, the crowd is going to go nuts. The ground is going to be shaking. They are definitely going to be yelling, and after the game, if you can still hear, you're going to be lucky."

Ultimately, the NCAA would once again weather the storm. Nobody committed suicide over the Manziel ruling, and at the end of the season it would be reported that more people attended college football games in the United States than in any other year in the history of the sport.

9

RICE

FINALLY, THE FOREVER that the Texas Aggie offseason football season had become was joyfully and mercifully approaching its conclusion. The months between actual on-the-field competition against another school had stretched into a seeming eternity during 2013. It had been an eight-month prison stretch for Aggie fans, and only for people actually behind bars did the days drag on more slowly.

Since accepting the Heisman Trophy and then dominating the AT&T Cotton Bowl Classic, Johnny Manziel had become a red-line item among the assembled ranks of the American sports media.

In the minds of every jock pundit in every market in the entire United States, the quarterback in College Station, Texas, had surpassed A-Rod for the uncoveted rank of America's Leading Lightning Rod. The Kerrville Kid had—through no intentional effort on his own part—been morphed by media mouths and laptops into a person who was part Hugh Hefner, part Charlie Sheen, with measures of Lindsay Lohan and Bernie Madoff tossed in as side embellishment.

Poor Johnny. A controversial tweet here, a premature departure from a football summer camp there—it was as if he couldn't send his mom flowers on her birthday without receiving a barrage of media criticism.

Flowers, eh? Was he drunk when sent the flowers? I'll bet he was. He had to have been because I, cohost of the *Bubba and Buck Show* on 107.8 AM sports radio right here in Irritable Bowel, Mississippi, said so. And who really paid for those? Probably some autograph broker in South Florida who also deals rocket launchers to A-rab terrorists. The NCAA will surely begin an investigation and, although I never jump to premature conclusions, will most certainly ban Manziel for life. Et cetera, et cetera. Blah, blah, blah.

That exact oration never happened, but plenty that were in the same reaches of absurdity certainly did. Had the noxious volumes of hot air expelled from broadcast journalists on the topic of Johnny Football been transformed into windmill energy, the entire nation and parts of Canada could have been lit up for a decade. Nobody in the Aggie fan base actually said so, but many had to have been relieved that attention shifted from Johnny's problems to the Boston Marathon bombings and the fertilizer explosion in West, Texas, because those events at least got Johnny out of the crosshairs of the Great American Information Machine for a couple of weeks.

On the Monday before the beginning of football season, one sonorous oracle of wisdom in the Dallas–Fort Worth market took to the radio airwaves and announced that throughout the upcoming Texas Aggie football campaign, he would keep Johnny Manziel "under [his] personal microscope."

At least one listener, who will remain unidentified, thought to himself, "Good. Because once the season finally starts, Manziel will stick your personal microscope so far up your ass, you'll be shittin' microscope parts until Halloween."

Finally, the Saturday of the Texas A&M football opener arrived. The visiting opponents were the Rice Owls from not-too-far-away Houston. It's about ninety or so miles to the south of the A&M, but when the wind comes up from the right direction, a person could stand atop the press box at Kyle Field and smell Houston. Well, they think it's Houston. The actual source of the foul air is a Houston suburb, Pasadena, which contains a bunch of petroleum refineries. Stink-adena is how people in Houston refer to the place. There is an Aggie joke about Stink-adena, but it is too vile and stupid to be repeated in this dignified volume.

When it comes to the identity of big-world cities, Houston stands out as about as blue collar and white trash as it gets—a "bourbon and trombone town," according one analyst of urban Americana during the 1940s. The ethos of the entire Texas Gulf Coast region could be summarized in a short, three-sentence story that appeared in the metro section of the *Houston Chronicle* in the 1980s that detailed a crime scene event in which a Houston-area man caught another guy in the act of having sexual intercourse with his horse. A gun fight ensued, and according to police reports, the horse was shot to death in the crossfire. The headline that topped the terse account of that event in the newspaper read, "Unbridled Passion Triggers Violence."

That is all anybody needs to know about Houston, Texas. Anyway, the kickoff of the Texas A&M–Rice game was scheduled for 2:30 p.m. Customarily, early-season football games in the state of Texas begin under the lights because, of course, not even mad dogs and Englishmen could survive the thermal excesses of a Lone Star afternoon in the late summertime.

This contest had been switched to a daylight setting because of a temple edict from national television. Every college football fan in the country would be interested in tuning into the Second Coming of the highly controversial Johnny Football. If any spectator dropped dead of heat stroke, Johnny Football would have been the man to blame. He would have been sued. You could have won a bet on that. Aggie athlete department officials, when they scheduled the Rice game five years ago, could not, in their wildest and most remote fantasies, have foreseen that a game against the Owls could generate so much hype, so much attention, and yes, even so much emotion.

The reason for that was simple enough. Nobody gives a damn about Rice football or Rice anything else when it comes to athletics, except possibly for former big-league all-star Lance Berkman, who went to school there.

Rice is one of those teams that the big boys of college football (and the middle-sized ones, too) schedule when they need to kick the living crap out of somebody. The big-time programs actually stand in line to schedule the Rice Owls. When the Owls go to Austin to get slaughtered by the Texas Longhorns, UT fans greet the Houston contingent with the chant, "What comes out of a Chinaman's ass?"

Rice is a school that doesn't really have much business even putting a team on the field—when it comes to intercollegiate competition, Rice is better suited for science fairs and chess. In a state populated by colleges of undistinguished academic accomplishment, no matter what their catalogs insist, Rice stands out as a community of rocket scientists, nanotechnologists, and eggheads.

The college is situated south of downtown Houston on a campus bedecked with tall red oak trees—a campus with gothic structures that could almost pass for Ivy League. The school has taken the cliché known as "higher learning" to extremes. Rice has produced 101 Fulbright scholars, eleven Truman scholars, twenty-four Marshall scholars, and twelve Rhodes scholars. When it comes to academic research in the field of material sciences, Rice is ranked first in the world. One can presume that the ranking was not bestowed by a panel of sportswriters on the weekly Associated Press poll.

While the football history of Rice could be summarized completely in a journal no thicker than a comic book, the background of the school itself is compelling. The college is named for its benefactor, William Marsh Rice, born in New England in 1816. Rice was a grocer who decided to seek a financial fortune in the primeval coastal community of Houston and was a visionary of every sort because the city was not, at the time, anything resembling a boomtown. But Marsh had a vision. He came, he saw, he prospered. He made his fortune in the conventional methods of his time—general store retail, lumber, railroads, and the like. At the beginning of the Civil War, he owned fifteen slaves.

Approaching the home stretch of his life on this planet, Rice moved to a Park Avenue residence in New York. Houston, after all, had been a humid place occupied by huge, blood-starved mosquitoes and largely uninhabitable for about eight months out of the year. He decided to devote much of his $4 million estate (worth at least $4 billion by contemporary standards) to the establishment of a school that would excel in literature and the scientific arts. Originally, he wanted to build an orphan asylum, but he later decided to go the school route.

Marsh died suddenly in 1900, and the day before his death, his will was altered. The entire estate would not go the construction of the college but rather—surprise, surprise—to his trusted lawyer, Albert T. Patrick, who, even back in that era, was upholding the customary standards of a distinguished officer of the court. Alas, the dumb shit did a sloppy job of forging Rice's signature on his big check, and a bank teller became suspicious.

The lawyer's scheme soon unraveled and Patrick went to prison, convicted of not only attempting to steal the estate of William Marsh Rice, but also for plotting his murder. Patrick's misdeeds were in some way, as they like to say within the profession, precedent setting. Henceforth, the first thing a student would learn in an American law school would be that when you murder your client and forge his signature, for Chrissakes, hire a professional.

So the school that William Marsh Rice had envisioned was indeed created to his specifications, although one must wonder if, in his boundless altruism, Rice had foreseen that the school that bore his name would participate in an activity as barbaric as football. Probably, the answer is yes, because even at the time of Rice's murder, the administrative overlords at learning establishments like Harvard, Yale, and Princeton had determined that a football team was one hell of a cash cow.

For decades the Rice Owls competed with limited success in the Southwest Conference, the coalition of Texas colleges that threw in Arkansas as well. The Hogs were invited to join the league because travelers to the Ozark State could avail themselves of the jars of homemade jam and pickle relish that were dispensed by little roadside stands along the state's major thoroughfares.

The football Owls did gain an element of notoriety during the post–World War II years because they were featured in an inordinate number of appearances on the Southwest Conference radio games of the week. The reason was that the person who announced the games, and selected the teams to appear was the immortal Kern Tips, whose actual day job was account executive at the TracyLocke ad agency in Houston. Tips hated to travel and would not unless he had to, so when the Owls played home games, they got on the statewide network.

It is fitting that the single most memorable play in the entire football history of the university was an aberration and an excursion into football infamy, an oddity that ranked right up there with the University of California's Roy Riegels' wrong-way run against Georgia Tech in the 1929 Rose Bowl game.

In 1953, the Owls, under coach Jess Neely, fielded a good team, featuring an even better running back named Dicky Moegle (changed in later years to the more phonetic "Maegle"). Moegle was a first-team All-American in an era when that was a big deal. Rice tied the Texas Longhorns for the Southwest Conference Championship and earned an invitation to play in the Cotton Bowl game because UT had appeared in the game the previous season. It should also be pointed out that during that time the New Year's bowl games were landmark events.

There were four: the Orange Bowl, the Sugar Bowl, the Cotton Bowl, and the Rose Bowl. Each game was televised—and during a time when college football fans were usually afforded a ration of one televised game a week during the regular season. So four games in one day amounted to an orgy for the gridiron enthusiasts, and New Year's became an annual event for which Dad could plop himself down in front of the family's faithful Philco TV set with its rabbit ears and twelve-inch black-and-white screen, get shit-faced, and watch football all day long.

"Honey! Take a break from the ironing, will ya, and bring me another beer."

The United States of America was never a greater place than it was on New Year's Day in the fifties.

So fans in the millions were gathered around their sets on January 1, 1954—a year during which, other than what took place in the Cotton Bowl, nothing of consequence happened. Google the year 1954 and it comes up blank.

Rice's appearance in the Dallas bowl game was hardly worthy of pre-game buildup, as it was the lesser of the four contests on the bowl-day agenda. The big game was the Rose Bowl matchup between UCLA and Michigan State. The Owls came into the game with an 8–2 regular-season record; the Crimson Tide, under Red Drew, had finished the season 5–2–3 (they had ties back in those days). 'Bama had opened the season with a shocking loss to Mississippi Southern, a school that gave new meaning to the concept of "backwater."

Still, the Tide had managed some ties against the better teams of the Southeastern Conference and upset the league champion, Georgia Tech, and it was on that basis that the team was invited to the Cotton Bowl game. 'Bama had a sophomore quarterback named Bart Starr, but he was better known that season for his skills as a punter and defensive back.

The contest was proceeding in routine fashion. Rice had taken the lead, 7–6, on a thirty-seven-yard TD run by Moegle. Alabama mounted a drive in the second quarter, but that ended when the Tide lost a fumble on the Owls' ten-yard line. A first-down offside violation pushed the Owls back to the five, and on the next play, it happened.

Moegle took a pitchout and took off around the right end. Rice's fullback leveled a linebacker, and Moegle, the fastest player on either team, sliced upfield, along the sideline, full-throttle with nothing but wide open spaces between him and the goal line. Moegle sprinted past the Alabama bench near midfield when—kabam—he went down like he'd been shot.

A phantom figure from the Baba bench, a player without a helmet, had illegally insinuated himself onto the playing field, flattened Moegle with a side-body block, and just as quickly vanished to the bench, where he attempted to conceal himself behind a teammate and a student trainer.

The guilty intruder turned out to be none other than Tommy Lewis, the Alabama team captain. Lewis, a God-fearin' son of the Alabama country raised on corn bread and butterbeans, had been overcome with old school pride and in an instantaneous and totally unpremeditated act, yielded to the urging of Satan to commit the heinous gridiron offense. And, in process of doing so, the Alabama Crimson Tide established a Twelfth Man tradition of its very own.

"I saw him coming, out of the corner of my eye, and turned away slightly, otherwise he might have broken my leg," Moegle reported after the game. "Still, he knocked the breath out of me and I was unable to get back on my feet for almost a full minute."

Moegle also remembered the high-pitched voice and highly Southern-accented protests of his coach, Neely, who confronted the 'Bama coach. "Red! Red! What's the meaning to this? Who in the world sent your boy on the field to tackle my boy?"

The referee, Cliff Shaw, had an unobstructed view of the entire calamity. While the football officials' handbook did not include any direct course of action in the event of a contingency like that one, Shaw decided on the spot to award Rice and Moegle the touchdown. The ninety-five yard run that ended prematurely with unscheduled stop still stands as the longest in Cotton Bowl history.

In a nation that at the time was starved for cheap thrills, the land had an overnight celebrity, and it wasn't Dickey Moegle. The following Sunday night, the star of the event, Lewis, appeared on *The Ed Sullivan Show*.

Given the background of the school, it remains appropriate that the most accomplished football player in the annals of the Rice Owls was a quarterback, Frank Ryan, who played for the Owls in the 1950s and eventually went on to start for the Cleveland Browns. Ryan, in fact, was the starter for the Cleveland Browns the last time the team won the National Football League championship in 1964 during the pre–Super Bowl era of pro football. That Cleveland team, coached by Paul Brown, was the beneficiary of a running back named Jim Brown.

Frank Ryan was a graduate of Paschal High School in Fort Worth. The year before the Browns' last title, he received his PhD. In physics. From Rice. His doctoral thesis was entitled *A Characterization of the Set of Asymptotic Values of a Function Holomorphic in the Unit Disc*. It was published in the *Duke Mathematical Journal*. At the time, Red Smith, a New York columnist and the first newspaper sportswriter to win a Pulitzer Prize, noted that the Browns' offense consisted of a quarterback who understood the theory of relativity and ten teammates who didn't know there was one.

But after Einstein-in-cleats graduated from Rice, the program descended more and more into a state of disrepair. The urgent transmission "Houston, we've got a problem" was initiated not by an astronaut aboard Apollo 13 but by Jess Neely and a procession of Rice football coaches. An ironic aspect of the Owls' gradual descent into the Nowheresville of college football is that the team played its home games in a seventy-two-thousand-seat arena that is perhaps unsurpassed in quality and design anywhere in college (or pro) athletics. Rice Stadium remains an architectural gem, a gorgeous red-brick double-decker completed in 1950. When it comes to sight lines, there is not a bad seat in the house. So Rice Stadium offers great views for the nonexistent persons in an empty grandstand.

In a historical footnote, when the NFL presented the 1975 Super Bowl game (Steelers vs. Vikings) to the huge and welcoming Sun Belt megalopolis of Houston, the spectacle was not conducted in the heralded Astrodome, home of the Oilers, but in the far more elegant home of the Rice Owls. The beautiful arena remains largely vacant and ignored.

The seasons for Rice limped past like wounded animals. By the 1970s, the school's fans on football Saturdays were attracted to the stadium more by the Rice band than the team itself. That band, which operated under the identity of the MOB (Marching Owl Band), gained some notoriety by presenting halftime shows that offered a satire of the opposing school. Satire, perhaps, is too mild a word. Insulting was more like it. Good taste was never an element in the band's presentation.

For instance, at a game at UT in 2007, after three Longhorns players had been arrested in separate off-campus events during the offseason, the MOB took the field and serenaded Texas fans with the theme from *Dragnet* while band members wearing UT jerseys were chased around the field by other band members inside cardboard police cars. All great stuff.

Aggies fans were less tolerant of parody. On one occasion in the dark past, the Owl band played "Where, Oh Where Has My Little Dog Gone" shortly after the passing of the A&M collie mascot. It got even worse when the MOB spoofed the Aggie band, at one point marching in goose step while the band's halftime announcer simulated a German accent: "You vill, of course, enjoy zee performance."

About a thousand Aggie cadets besieged the musicians, who barricaded themselves beneath the stadium.

Thus, in a sport that draws heavily on the memories and events of all things past, the 2013 A&M–Rice season opener was, thanks to the celebrity of Johnny Manziel, thrust into a strange spotlight. Kyle Field, with nearly one hundred thousand faithful generating a roaring racket that vibrated throughout the Brazos bottoms of south-central Texas, sat patiently through the first half awaiting the conclusion of their hero's two-quarter suspension imposed by the highest authority of the National Collegiate Athletic Association.

The crowd's sense of anticipation was visceral during the first half while Manziel's stand-in, Matt Joeckel, enjoyed some moments of stardom of his own. Joeckel was the twin brother of offensive tackle Luke Joeckel, Johnny Football's main man from the 2012 team who had departed to Jacksonville after being selected as the No. 2 overall pick in the NLF draft. His younger (by a matter of a couple of minutes) brother led the Maroon-clads to four first-half touchdowns. The rub was that the inexperienced Texas A&M defense appeared way too porous at times and yielded three TDs to the unheralded Feathered Flock from Houston. Halftime score: Ags 28, Owls 21. Translation: not good.

Ah, but that second half. The old Civil War tune "When Johnny Comes Marching Home" had long served as a staple in the Aggie band's repertoire, but it never seemed so resounding, so moving, than when Manziel, emancipated at last from the tyrannies of the NCAA enforcement branch, loped onto the field.

A little rust was evident at first. But only a little. After his first drive ended with a field goal, Manziel quickly reverted to his Heisman form of 2012. He threw down three TD passes in rapid succession. he highlight of Johnny's grand reentry happened in the third quarter when he mimicked himself signing an autograph for a Rice defender.

Johnny's message to the NCAA and the legion of wailing media critics: stick it.

Later, Manziel got flagged for an unsportsmanlike conduct call after trash talking a Rice player.

Kevin Sumlin promptly pulled him. After the game, he said all of the politically correct things about Manziel needing to demonstrate more maturity, but he made sure not to lay it on too thick. Thanks to that player who needed to demonstrate maturity, he was being mentioned as a candidate for jobs that extended from USC to the National Football League.

Bottom line: Texas A&M 52, Rice 31.

Said Aggie offensive lineman Cedric Ogbuehi of the Manziel antics that seemed to agitate his coach: "He is going to be loud and aggressive. That's what makes him Johnny Football. That's how he is. He's a fiery guy and that's why we love him."

Rice had to love him, too. Thanks to Manziel, the Owls received the most exposure they had enjoyed since Tommy Lewis tackled Dickey Moegle sixty years earlier. Buoyed by the elixir of backdoor fame, the Owls went to win the Conference USA championship and appear in a bowl game for the first time since the Kennedy administration.

Aggies fans, after the game, piled into the bistros along the north end of the campus for cold refreshment where they would be confronted with wall-to-wall arrangements of plasma television screens. And on those screens, or most of them, were the Alabama Crimson Tide, opening its season in a game that began an hour or so after the Aggies had finished beating Rice.

'Bama was playing a team substantially more formidable than the Owls. That was Virginia Tech, a team that season after season has shown a propensity for being not quite good enough to appear in the top ten rankings, but was frequently located in a slot between eleven and twenty. The Hokies and the Tide were playing at a neutral site, which was Atlanta's Georgia Dome. That happened to qualify as 'Bama's home away from home, as it was the site of the annual Southeastern Conference postseason championship game.

Aggies gazed the set, and universally pulled for Virginia Tech, although not too loudly. Everybody in College Station—every football fan in the United States—realized that the Hokies did not have a prayer against the Crimson Crusaders in all of their No. 1 grandeur. The final score seemed close enough, 28–10, but Nick Saban's troops racked up their twenty-eight quick, then largely took the rest of the day off.

The real trial was coming just two weeks later, to the day, at College Station, and by then the fans of both schools were counting not the hours, but the minutes and seconds. Tick, tick, tick. Alabamans largely felt that was to be their game of the season. Aggies, on the other hand, viewed the confrontation as the Maroon and White game of the century. True, the century was only thirteen years old. But if Aggies won that game, it could resonate for the full one hundred.

The A&M–Alabama game now took on the menacing specter of a Category 5 hurricane that had formed in the hot salt water seas of the Caribbean and was heading toward the U.S. mainland. But in College Station, nobody was making any evacuation plans.

10

SAM HOUSTON STATE

LOOKING CRISP, BLOND, cheerful, and tidy, a contingent of four exuberant young people occupied a booth near the heart of the collegiate-urban sprawl that the Texas A&M campus has become. The quartet—two women and two men—radiated a visceral vibe of joy and eternal hope.

They greeted strolling student Aggies—and anyone else who happened to be prowling the premises—with handshakes and radiant smiles. A sign above their location read, "Howdy. I'm a Mormon."

It was expedient that the small spirit delegation, otherwise known as the Latter-Day Saints, let it be known they were in College Station on missionary service. That work is required of all students at Brigham Young University, who take a year or two off to visit locations like Togo and Borneo to spread the word of the good news that accompanies their theology. Texas A&M lacks the third-world credentials to attract relief work—whether it be Mormon, the Red Cross, the United Nations, or the Peace Corps.

College Station has enjoyed the benefits of indoor plumbing for several decades now, and the incidence of smallpox, tuberculosis, black plague, and the like is rare in the precincts where many people are clad in maroon T-shirts. Residents of Brazos County seldom die of starvation. No, the Mormons had visited the campus to stir up enthusiasm, offer enlightenment, and perhaps enlist some new converts.

But the sign atop their booth broadcast the fact that these young people knew exactly where they were, and it was not Central Africa or Haiti or New Guinea. They understood that they were deep in the deepest heart of Texas, and furthermore, they knew that in order to get along with a Texan, the first thing one must do is talk like a Texan.

You have to sprinkle your regular conversational patterns with little terms like, "I'll ya one thing, buddy" or "That dog won't hunt" or "No shit?" It is not known whether the A&M on-campus Mormon delegations resort to those extremes, but that simple "Howdy" demonstrated that this group was traveling along the correct path. Aggies use that word a whole lot, along with a refinement of it: "Hi-di."

So, while the post–Labor Day 2013 atmosphere of College Station was, as usual, enshrouded with all things Texan—right down to its non-Texan Mormons—the football schedule announced that the Aggies' upcoming opponent came from a point of origin that could be reached, round trip, for about five dollars' worth of the gas in the old Dodge Ram pickup truck.

That was Sam Houston State University in Huntsville, located just fifty or so miles east of the College Station–Bryan area. Sam Houston State calls itself the Bearkats and they are not nationally known as a college football powerhouse. This is a Division II operation and fairly typical of the sorts of teams that currently and conveniently occupy the schedules of the all major college football industrial powerhouses. Same old story. Christians versus Lions. Everybody loves a good, healthy slaughter, especially the lions.

This Sam Houston State matchup had at least demonstrated some creative accomplishment on the part of the schedule maker. (That's got to be a great racket. Terrific job. What does your daddy do? He's a schedule maker. The dough ain't that great, but you can't beat the hours.) Bearkats and Aggies. They drank the same beer, ate the same barbeque, slept with one another's spouses. Throughout the years, Sam Houston State has produced a lengthy array of notable graduates. Well, at least two.

One of them was the motion picture actor Dana Andrews, who appeared in one of greatest Hollywood films of all time, *The Best Years of Our Lives*. Another product of Sam Houston State was Dan Rather. The school's football program has had over a dozen players appear on NFL rosters. The most notable of those, however, was Guido Merkens, who is best remembered for being named Guido Merkens.

This is in no way intended to cast aspersions on Sam Houston State or the galaxy of other lower-classification college teams across the nation. The Academy of Arts Urban Knights of San Francisco, the Southern Arkansas Muleriders of Magnolia, the South Dakota School of Mines Hardrockers of Rapid City, and the Lincoln Memorial Railsplitters of Harrogate, Tennessee, are proud schools that compete in leagues such as the Peach Belt Conference and the Heartland Conference and the Sunshine State Conference. Products of these kinds of off-Broadway citadels of academics gain every bit as much meaningful lifetime preparation as the students at the UCLAs, Michigan States, and the like.

The only drawback is that it's tougher to advance to the top graduate programs in medicine and law and business from these smaller points of origin, even with a four-point GPA.

So there was no real stigma attached to the No. 6 ranked team in college football taking on a challenge from Sam Houston State. The appeal of this matchup, limited as it was, happened to be the fact that the Bearkats come from the only place even more Texan than College Station. That would be the town of Huntsville, not largely known outside of the state—or inside it, in some cases. Huntsville natives do not necessary claim the distinction of Most Texan Town in Texas. It just is, and the reasons why require some explanation.

Motorists driving Interstate 45, the well-traveled thoroughfare that connects Dallas and Houston, are, if they making that journey for the first time, startled by the appearance of a manmade apparition that appears seemingly out of nowhere among the tall pines that proliferate along the roadside on the south edge of Huntsville, rather nearer to Houston than Dallas.

It's a statue, a towering white work of art that depicts a strange-looking man attired in an even stranger-looking suit of clothes. It is a sixty-seven-foot-tall replica of Sam Houston, and when we say the thing materializes out of nowhere, we mean just that. There are no billboards informing drivers "Five Miles Ahead to Statue of Sam Houston" and other such warnings that usually advertise the fact that a potential tourist attraction lies up the road ahead.

No, this unannounced visual attraction has supplied many WTF moments to millions of wayfarers. An artist named David Adickes (a Sam Houston State grad, by the way) created the work, which was completed in 1994. Certain aficionados of U.S. history contend that his work more closely resembles P. T. Barnum than old Sam. Each man wore these mutton-chop sideburns that seemed so popular in the late sixties—both the 1860s and the 1960s.

Information in the gift shop hidden near the base of the towering rendition of General Houston reveals that this is the world's tallest free-standing statue of an American hero. (It does not say whether, somewhere on the planet, there is a taller free-standing statue of an American scumbag.) Gift shop propaganda grudgingly concedes that the Sam Houston statue, in height, stands second only to what the gift shop proprietors refer to as the "overpromoted" Statue of Liberty, which, upon close inspection, looks like some guy in drag.

What also could be drawn into play is a discussion of the subjective criteria that determines who qualifies for the label of hero. Throughout the nineteenth century, the true definition of a Texas hero was a sociopath who got kicked out of someplace respectable east of the Mississippi River. Sam Houston was certainly well-tailored for that role.

His statue depicts the great man leaning on a cane. Perhaps that was the same cane that Sam Houston used to whip the living crap out of a political foe, fellow congressman William Stanberry of Ohio, on a Washington, D.C., street in 1830. In a proceeding that was held to censure Houston for the assault, he was defended by Francis Scott Key. Sam lost, and it is doubtful that Rep. Stanberry felt that Houston rated the rank of hero.

The same was true of Sam Houston's wife. Well, she never actually functioned as his wife, but rather, as a person who participated in a marriage ceremony with him. Houston got married at the urging of his Tennessee political mentor, Andrew Jackson. Old Hickory suggested to Sam that if he wished to get far in politics, he needed to be married. Otherwise, people might mistake him for a hairdresser or something.

So Sam convinced a woman named Eliza Allen to become his bride. Eliza wasn't just any woman, by the way, but the educated and refined product of a well-known family.

Sam and Eliza spent their wedding night at the home of a prominent couple in Nashville. Early the next morning, Sam was occupied in a snowball fight with two little daughters of the host and hostess.

"You should go out and help Sam," the hostess laughingly told Eliza. "He seems to be losing the snowball fight."

"I hope they kill him," said Eliza.

"Oh, surely you are joking," interjected the hostess.

"No, I mean it from the bottom of my heart," Eliza responded. "I hope they kill him."

The wedding night was the first and last one that Eliza and Sam would spend in intimate company. Rumor and speculation—two commodities with which Johnny Manziel had become so familiar in 2013—surrounded the breakup and subsequent divorce of Mr.

and Mrs. Houston. Some would contend that the bride was repulsed by the spectacle of Sam Houston naked; he had sustained some wounds during his campaign against the Creek Indians that, well, looked kind of gross. Others circulated the theory that Eliza was less than turned on when Sam attempted to "introduce her to some of the exotic sexual activities" that he had learned from ladies of the night in New Orleans during his service under Andrew Jackson in the War of 1812. It was that kind of talk that eventually compelled Houston to get the hell away from Tennessee forever and come to Texas. Bill Clinton only *thought* he had it bad.

While Sam and Eliza proved incompatible, Sam and Texas were made for each other. Among his pals in the Cherokee tribes, Sam was given a name that, when translated from their Native American language, meant "the Big Drunk." His place in Texas history was secured when he led the Texas forces to a resounding victory over the Mexican army at the Battle of San Jacinto. In his memoirs, Mexican general Santa Ana reported that upon surrendering to Sam Houston he was certain that he would be placed immediately in front of a firing squad. Instead, Houston poured Santa Ana a drink and then hopefully asked if he had any opium on him.

Sam Houston's legacy resounds even into modern times. During the 1980s, Massachusetts senator Edward Kennedy visited Austin, Texas, and was given red carpet treatment by the governor at the time, Mark White. That included a tour of the governor's mansion.

According to Robert Mann, who served as the senator's press secretary, White escorted Kennedy into an upstairs bedroom and declared, "It is here, Mr. Kennedy, according to legend, that Sam Houston himself consorted with Cherokee Indian prostitutes."

To which Teddy cheerfully asked, "Are there any on the premises now?"

The town of Huntsville is the site of the statue and a college named in Sam Houston's honor because that's where he chose to live the latter years of his life. (He's also buried there.) The college was founded in 1879 and is the third oldest in the state. Legend has it that the college was originally to be called the Sam Houston Institute of Technology, but the founding fathers rejected the idea after considering the acronym.

There are other reasons that Huntsville qualifies for the designation of Most Texan. It happens to be the home of the oldest Texas state prison, formally known as the Texas State Penitentiary at Huntsville, which houses the most active execution chamber in the United States.

Make no mistake. The story of Texas is a story of violence and a story of death, and that's a story that begins and ends with its prison legacy.

The Texas criminal justice system started killing people as soon as the state was admitted to the union. Many of the earlier executions involved individuals convicted of piracy, treason, and, during the Civil War, desertion. Later, those on the receiving end of the vengeance of the state were exclusively found guilty of murder or rape. The prevailing method of departure was the hangman's noose until 1923, when the electric chair was ushered in as a concession to the modern era of technology. This device went by a couple of friendly aliases, like Old Sparky and the Hot Squat. It was situated in a room referred to by prison guards as the dance hall.

On opening night, five inmates, including two brothers, got fried. A lawmaker who introduced the bill that originally financed the chair was an invitee to watch the device in action on the occasion of its formal debut. He was so horrified by what he witnessed that he rushed back to Austin to plead with fellow legislators to shut down the device. Old Sparky was clearly not as humane as he had been led to believe. The stench alone was enough to make you puke. Well. Tough shit. Faint of heart is not a characteristic conducive to advancement in the arts and sciences of Texas politics.

Old Sparky would finally be retired after four decades of distinguished service. After killing 363 people, he deserved a rest. (Author's note: person 341 on Sparky's list, Fred Leath, was prosecuted in Fort Worth by the author's father. Leath was a gay guy who was convicted of killing an eighteen-year-old boy who attempted to roll him. Self-defense was argued. The prosecutor, my old man, did not insist on a death penalty, but the jury issued it anyway. So my father unsuccessfully pled clemency for Leath in a hearing before the Texas Court of Criminal Appeals and then resigned his job as a prosecutor. The author learned of these events while in college, when he was surprised to read about them in the Austin newspaper.)

Inmates no longer die in the electric chair. They are done in via lethal injection while lying prone on what is known in the death house as the "journey gurney." Never let it be said that Texas prison culture lacks a sense of humor. Currently, the population of Texas' death row exceeds that of the entire state of Vermont. (Well, that might be stretching it some, but you get the point.)

Life for those destined to remain living behind those storied Texas walls is no springtime picnic in the park. This author interviewed some inmates a few years ago for a magazine article. A man named Andrew was described by authorities as a model inmate. Twenty-eight years before, he had been convicted as a juvenile of killing a store clerk during a robbery. He was soon to be paroled.

Once I get out, if I should encounter anybody, and I mean anybody, who I had known in here, I'll run and hide under a car or something. You've gotta remember, these guys aren't in here for singing too loud in church. This place is brutal. Every day they get up at 3 a.m. to work in the cotton fields that have guards with mirrored sunglasses, carrying shotguns, on horseback, just like in the movies. Except that the horses are meaner than the guards. They're trained to bite the shit out you. At least I have one big advantage out there. I'm not afraid of snakes.

Another interviewee, identified by those same authorities as anything *but* a model prisoner, was named Chico. As a youth,

Chico said he began his criminal career stealing nickel candies and soon graduated to "jacking jewelry." Chico maintained the torso and demeanor of the prototypical Southeastern Conference player he might have become had he not run afoul of the cops. In prison, Chico bitched about everything. Especially, life in "ad seg," which was by then what they called solitary confinement. "In regular prison, you're a bird in a cage. In ad seg, you're a bug in a matchbox. But in the long run, prison is like any other place. Boys will be boys and boys will be girls," he said. That was another source of Chico's bitterness against life both in and out of the prison system.

"My brother was a schoolteacher, a straight dude, but he died of AIDS. Got if off a bitch. Me? I been fuckin' punks in here for ten years and never caught nothing. Where's the justice? Where's the justice?"

This information is pertinent to the gridiron to the very real extent that several of the Sam Houston State players Johnny Manziel and the Texas Aggies would confront in their final dress rehearsal for the Alabama game were already moonlighting as guards at various prison facilities in and around Huntsville. Mostly, they were lineman, pursuing degrees in criminal justice and salaried careers behind the razor wire, tending to the security of the population of the people outside and protecting the people on the inside from one another.

On the football field, of course, these athletes would not be carrying bludgeons or shotguns or be mounted on top of inmate-hating horses. But they were armed with mean dispositions and biceps the size of the beer kegs and were, therefore, worthy of respect.

Still, the challenge that confronted coach Kevin Sumlin was not that his team would be flat as diet cola, but guarding against the very real possibility that Johnny Football and company might rack up a hundred points. The Las Vegas line had opened with the Aggies listed as forty-five point favorites. The task of artfully holding down a score without actually insulting an opponent like Sam Houston State is not as easy as it might seem. It required supplying the illusion of going full blast, while at the same, keeping the game clock running as much and as long as possible. Even on the opening possession, ball carriers were implored to stay inbounds.

Manziel helped some by throwing an interception on Texas A&M's second possession. He was in a tricky spot. Tossing the occasional pick against an opponent like the Bearkats served as a harmless or even worthwhile endeavor. But at end of the campaign, the Heisman voters, many of them card-carrying members of the Children of Mindlessly, would peer at the overall season stats and factor those into their ballot choices, regardless of the circumstances under which the numbers were registered.

Sam Houston State did its part by moving the ball and occasionally scoring against the Aggie defense, which exposed its own inexperience in the opener against Rice and did so at times against the Kats. The defense was also watered down to some extent with the absence of three customary starters who were serving in-house suspensions for transgressions against team rules.

Actually, the heavy underdogs cut the Aggies lead to 30–21 after the first minute of the second half, and then the dam burst, just as everyone in the stadium knew it would. Manziel departed the scene in the third quarter, giving way to true freshman Kenny Hill, a lad blessed with a future unlimited.

The final score was 65–28. Willie Fritz, the Bearkats coach, said the Aggie offense was "one of the best I have ever seen," and added needlessly, "We could not stop them. We have some defensive linemen who could stand to be twenty or thirty pounds heavier."

While the Aggies were dismantling the Bearkats, the Crimson Tide had been working against a tougher opponent. They were practicing against themselves, since their September 7 Saturday was of an off-week.

Sumlin could consider the Sam Houston State project a success, basically. The Aggies held the score well under one hundred and in the process incurred no injuries that would affect the team in their game against Alabama.

As for Sam Houston State, the Bearkats could safely return to the peace of nonexistence in the NCAA Division II workplace and a schedule that included the more reasonable likes of Nicholls State, Central Arkansas, and Incarnate Word. Their appearance before an audience at Kyle Field, which exceeded ninety thousand, was by far the largest to witness a Sam Houston State game, and that gained a payday for the university that would certainly enable it to continue producing some of the best damn prison guards in the entire damn world.

11

ALABAMA GAME

CULTURALLY AND HISTORICALLY, Texas stands out as the American Australia.

However, settlers didn't arrive as alleged criminal miscreants wearing leg irons, destined for a lifetime in a penal colony. They came as opportunists seeking prosperity in a territory untamed and unregulated. Such an adventurer, to select one at random, was Charles Alderson, a pharmacist who came to Waco in 1885. He created a soda fountain concoction heavily laced with prune juice. Customers loved the stuff, a laxative that was tasty and refreshing.

Soon, Alderson began bottling and distributing his creation. He decided to name the product after his former employer back in Virginia, who had invited him to leave the state after discovering that Alderson was having an affair with his daughter. The man's name was Dr. Pepper.

Another such visionary was William George Crush, a longtime employee of the Missouri-Kansas-Texas (Katy) railroad. Crush was a dreamer and conceived the brainstorm that became the first major outdoor entertainment event in the state. It was a train wreck. Crush convinced Katy management that a production like that would work as a marvelous promotional device for the railroad. This was in 1896. His bosses could not argue.

Two gigantic steam locomotives, behemoths, horses of iron that had been designated for retirement, were selected to perform as stars of the show. They were known as Old 999 and Old 1001, Class 44D locomotives, the renowned "big eight-wheelers." Each was equipped with two pilot axles and two drive axles. One was painted bright red, the other olive green, and they chugged across the state for weeks while stirring up excitement for the amazing event.

Special tracks were constructed outside of Waco, and an instant town, Crush, Texas, was incorporated as the site. Special Katy passenger trains were chartered to bring in train wreck fans from all over Texas; the cars were so crowded that many persons rode on the roofs of the cars as they arrived in Crush. Bleacher seats were rented from the Ringling Brothers people to accommodate the spectators. At game time, over forty thousand people were assembled, and Crush was, for a day at least, the eighth largest city in Texas.

It was September 16, and the show was delayed for one hour while cops pressed the crowd back into an area they assumed would be a safe distance from the collision. Each locomotive would pull seven box cars loaded with railroad ties. At 5 p.m., two engineers blew the shrieking steam-generated whistles, locked the throttles into the full-forward position, and leaped from the cabs of the locomotives. The steam engines would collide head-on at a combined speed of 120 miles an hour. The resulting mayhem was all that the promoters had envisioned—only more so. Pop-off valves on both engines failed to function, and the boilers of both locomotives unexpectedly exploded, catapulting large chunks of hot metal hundreds of feet into the air.

Two spectators died on the spot, another the following day, and dozens were injured by the debris and the shrapnel, many seriously. A professional photographer lost an eye to a flying bolt. According to a news report at the time, the Katy railroad paid off the damage claims of the injured "as soon as they were presented."

The railroad also fired George Crush, but rehired him the next day. Scott Joplin, the immortal ragtime musician, wrote a song about the fiasco, "The Great Crash at Crush," and that became one of his first major successes.

The old timers who traffic in Texas folklore—well, one of them—developed a theory that the nuclear-grade explosion from the train wreck extended into outer space and was the source of the state's first major UFO event. A flying saucer, he claimed, came to investigate the source of the commotion.

Well, in 1897 a strange airship did apparently encounter engine trouble and the cigar-shaped craft crashed into a water tower on a ranch in Aurora, Texas, in the northern portion of Parker County west of Fort Worth. The wreckage contained a being who was killed. The body was badly charred and mangled, and the *Dallas Morning News*, which offered page-one exposure of the event, reported it was plain that "the pilot was not a resident of this world." The story noted that the townspeople provided the alien with a "Christian burial" in the Aurora cemetery. That funeral must have been a doozie.

"O heavenly father, please grant eternal peace to our departed brother . . . uh . . . Zoltan . . ."

As far as UFO events go, the Aurora happening ranks right up with what allegedly occurred in Roswell, New Mexico, exactly fifty years later. An official Texas historical marker that tells the tale stands at the gate of the Aurora cemetery, and the alien creature's gravestone is adorned with a chiseled likeness of the spaceship.

The Crash at Crush may or may not have attracted space ships to Texas, but it might be effectively argued that the train wreck served as a precursor to eventual outdoor exhibitions that became known as college football games. Any coach in Texas will quickly confirm that football is, after all, a collision sport.

And so, 116 years later, almost to the day, the long-awaited Texas A&M–Alabama football game could well have been billed as the

Crash at College Station. The contest had been sold out for almost a year, or not long after the occasion when the Aggies pulled their stirring upset of the Crimson Tide in the 2012 game in Tuscaloosa.

The only person within the ranks of the athletic department at A&M under more pressure than coach Kevin Sumlin was Alan Cannon, the sports information director, or SID. He was assigned the task of granting media credentials to the avalanche of reporters who were beyond eager to cover a game in which the winner would own a clear inside track to the BCS Championship Game, which was scheduled the following January at the Rose Bowl in Pasadena, California. Cannon would be hard-pressed to find a place to put them all. Even more stressful was the duty of declining the media requests of the smaller outlets, the little weekly papers that used to constitute the backbone of American journalism.

Alan Cannon's publicity department at Texas A&M included about a dozen full-time assistants, plus an additional ample squad of student part-timers. What a departure that was from SID operations in the sixties and early seventies when this author worked as a newspaper sportswriter. During that time, the SID staff consisted of one guy, who usually shared his office with a coed who would come and stuff his weekly press release into envelopes and carry them to the post office. The SIDs of that era usually came equipped with a personality that matched those of the sportswriters—in other words, a lush. The SID usually had experience working in a newspaper sports department. Around the Southwest Conference, the SID ranks consisted of a grand cast of characters. Jim "Hoss" Brock at TCU has been previously described. A leading counterpart was Jones Ramsey at Texas, the self-proclaimed "world's tallest fat man." Ramsey made certain that his game day press box buffet consisted of the best Tex-Mex cuisine available in all of Austin.

Bill Whitmore at Rice was memorable, if nothing else, for a face that was so red, it could be seen at night from miles away, like neon in Las Vegas. At SMU, little Junior Eldridge took writers for swell Italian meals at an alleged mob joint near the campus. Its owner supposedly provided a lift to downtown Dallas for the alleged shooter on the grassy knoll on November 22, 1963.

At Texas A&M, a tall, thin, and taciturn man named Spec Gammon made sure that writers were given VIP access to a little joint on the outskirts of College Station that served what was arguably the best barbeque in Texas, and if so, then therefore inarguably the best barbeque on the planet Earth.

Sportswriters used to find any excuse not to travel all the way to Lubbock to cover Texas Tech games. Lubbock is a West Texas city that performs a stunningly good impersonation of the dark side of the moon. But Tech SID Ralph Carpenter took visiting scribes to a restaurant called the Gridiron that featured T-bone steaks nearly two inches thick. Carpenter was a relentlessly jolly character, who, as the saying went, never met a stranger. He liked to introduce himself to people and then inquire, "Got any nekkid pictures of your mother? Want to buy some?"

The real task of the SID was to arrange hospitality events for visiting media the evenings before football games, and if the game was a daytime affair, another party on the nights following the games. It was at these soirees that the scribes would get knee-crawling drunk and behave atrociously. On one celebrated occasion, SMU's traveling media party visited the Air Force Academy in Colorado Springs, where the pre-game festivities took place in the home of the commandant. The commandant's wife played the role of the gracious hostess, and one overserved media representative from Dallas mistook the nature of her charming congeniality and pressed his hotel room key into her hand.

Right away, she showed the key to the commandant himself and said, "Look what that man just gave me." The commandant was so amused that he instructed two military cops to escort the Texan outside, where they proceeded to beat the living shit out of him. Those were the days—long ago and vanished forever.

With the advent of the 1980s, the function and demeanor of the college SID would change into something more stern, more big-businesslike, in part because the field of sportswriting had become transformed from the so-called toy department into something more resembling hardcore journalism, some of it of the investigative kind. During the time when the Texas Aggies were residing atop the football world of the Southwest Conference under the coaching leadership of Jackie Sherrill, an employee of a car dealership in Arlington, Texas, surreptitiously videotaped a transaction in which an Aggie football assistant coach bought a Corvette for a hotshot recruit. The guy then took his video and showed it to the sports editor of the *Fort Worth Star-Telegram*, James Walker. So Walker then dispatched one his best writers, Whit Canning, to travel to College Station and get an explanation from Sherrill himself.

Whit Canning was, and still is, a top-shelf writer and a helluva person. I had worked with Canning a decade previously at the *Fort Worth Press*, where the editor-in-chief was, on his good days, a meddler and a pain in the ass. One morning, Whit received a phone call in which he was informed that his mother had just died. Realizing that he was about to come into some substantial funds from his mother's estate, Canning, without hesitation, walked into the office of the newspaper editor, told the editor to fuck himself, walked out of the building, and never came back. For the next several years, he stationed himself beside the swimming pool at his apartment and sipped scotch. You could find him out there in the middle of a sleet storm.

Finally, his inheritance ran out and Canning was obligated to return to writing sports, which was why he found himself having lunch in College Station with Jackie Sherrill himself in the Aggies dining hall at a time when NCAA investigators were often frequent visitors at A&M. Canning recalled the incident with relish: "When I finally got around to informing ol' Jackie about the actual reason for my visit, he really busted a gasket and cussed me out big time.

"Then I told him about the video and told him that he could watch if he wanted to. Jackie got silent for a moment or two, and then he asked me the name of the car dealership. I told him and then he said, 'Well, I'll tell you one goddamn thing. That's the last fuckin' Chevrolet they'll ever sell to a Texas Aggie! Want some more pie?'"

Of course, that was during a time when national championships were not won on the actual playing field, but on the showroom floors of car dealerships. Amid the modern coaching landscape of the heavy operators like the Nick Sabans and Kevin Sumlins, the football programs no longer buy new cars for promising high school athletes. They have found it much more cost effective to take out four-year leases. Also, no coach will ever again be caught red-handed on a car lot. Nowadays, those transactions are conducted online.

The long-awaited week had arrived at last. On the Thursday before the Saturday that would rock the football world, that crimson fleet, the Alabama armada that contained the Roll Tide faithful, was crossing the Texas state line in their hotels on wheels bound for College Station. There they would park in their designated area and start banging down those pure-grain-alcohol 'Bama Bombers. Persons of the Roll Tide persuasion are a bit like the old-time sportswriters in that when their blood alcohol levels reach the mid-.2 level, they are inclined to become pejorative. Those kinds of writers are long extinct. The last of that breed in Texas was afforded endangered species protection from the state game and fish commission, but a hunter killed the old scribe after mistaking him for a feral hog.

But there was no shortage of Roll Tide people in College Station. Campus officials were concerned, and with good reason, about potential ugliness between the Alabama campers and the Aggies football faithful, who were endowed with some qualities of rowdiness in their own right. The Aggies officials offered the same stern warnings to the students that people receive when they enter Yellowstone Park. They were to avoid the Tide people like Yellowstone tourists are instructed by park rangers to avoid encounters with bears and moose. Do not approach them. Photograph them, but only from a safe distance, and for God's sake, don't try to feed them anything.

Nothing of a serious nature occurred between the people wearing crimson and the ones decked out in maroon in the hours leading up to the football conflagration, at least nothing that was media-worthy. In a way, this football game shaped up as something similar to the NASCAR Sprint Cup season. (By the way, when is it finally going to dawn on the NCAA that collegiate stock-car racing would be tantamount to a license to print money, at least in the SEC and ACC?) The most important race, the Daytona 500, was always the leadoff event, and everything that followed was anticlimactic. In College Station, on a day that was not quite mid-September, no media person, no football pundit, would suggest that the upcoming event wouldn't indeed serve as the college football game of the season, a contest that would overshadow even the BCS title match.

Here it finally was. While Johnny Manziel had experienced his offseason of discontent, the same period had not been exactly a time of sunshine and roses in Tuscaloosa. Four Tide players had been charged with robbing two students, beating them into unconsciousness in a dormitory, stealing their iPhones and credit cards, and using those cards to buy items out of vending machines. Nick Saban issued a statement revealing that his program didn't condone that kind of cheap shit. They would "no longer be part of the program." Too bad. They were freshmen and had a damn good upside.

Also, Alabama's returning star quarterback, A. J. McCarron, considered a real threat to Johnny Manziel's aspirations of winning back-to-back Heisman Trophies, had been relegated to second-string celebrity status, one rung beneath his girlfriend, Katherine Webb.

McCarron had ABC play-by-play man Brent Musburger to thank for that. While 'Bama was thrashing Notre Dame in the process of winning its national championship, the TV cameras showed a closeup of Webb. Musburger was overcome by the young woman's loveliness. Seemingly unable to control himself, Musburger managed to come across as something of a dirty old man. To Musburger's credit, when the criticism poured in from the conventional places, he remained mostly unapologetic.

The publicity landed Webb a job modeling in the swimsuit issue of *Sports Illustrated*. Musburger could rightfully have claimed half her fee. After all, he'd put her on the map. Webb was in the stands during a CBS telecast of an Alabama game during the 2013 season and once again received closeup camera treatment.

"There is Katherine Webb, who dates the Alabama quarterback," said the announcer, Verne Lundquist.

"Is that all you're going to say?" chimed in telecast partner Gary Danielson.

"You're darned right it is," was Lundquist's response.

Lundquist and Danielson were on the air waves again in College Station. As the Alabama kicker placed the football on the tee to open the proceedings, Lundquist noted a weather forecast said that "a cold front" would blow through the area around game time. "And so it has," said Verne, who got his first big sportscasting job at the ABC affiliate in Dallas hosting *Bowling for Dollars*. "Over the last two hours, the temperature has dropped from ninety-six degrees all the way to ninety-two."

So the Crash at College Station was underway, but unlike the train wreck, where two steam locomotives, Old 999 and Old 1001, had been the stars, this football event essentially could be refined into a contest between two quarterbacks. Manziel was characterized by his spontaneous explosive qualities. McCarron's approach was more akin to the old baseball player Wee Willie Keeler's: "Hit 'em where they ain't."

The opening kickoff sailed all the way through the end zone for a touchback, like they almost always do in modern football, either pro or college, and Johnny trotted onto the field. Surrounded by a howling Kyle Field mob and being watched by the biggest TV audience to tune into a regular-season college game since 2006, Manziel somehow appeared calm and casual, like grandpa walking up to the corner drug store to buy a pack of Kools. Johnny Football was a young man who, as Kipling wrote, kept his head when all those around him were losing theirs.

On the first play from scrimmage, Johnny took off on a designed running play, took advantage of a block from his running back Ben Malena, and gained eleven yards. Gig 'em! In blinding sunlight, it was a beautiful life in Aggieland. Next play, Manziel retreated and passed down the sideline to Mike Evans, who raced along to the front of the Aggies bench into Alabama territory, a gain of more than thirty yards.

Evans, at six-foot-five and equipped with an astoundingly long arm, was using the showcase to plainly determine that in the fall of 2014 he would be making his living playing on Sunday, and by that we don't mean the organ at the College Station assembly. Mike Evans was a stud. He caught another pass for the Aggie offense with a gimme putt off the Alabama goal line, and Crimson Tide defensive coaches realized that their shorter defensive backs (like the player with the greatest name in the history of college football, Ha Ha Clinton-Dix) would stand no chance in this game if they persisted in attempting to hold Evans in check with man-to-man single coverage. Defensive coordinator Kirby Smart made certain that adjustments were quickly being put into place.

Manziel notched the game's first touchdown with a fluttering pass to Cameron Clear near the back of the end zone. Just one short year ago, Cameron Clear was playing before audiences of practically nobody for a junior college team in Yuma, Arizona. He was out there in exile after being kicked off the team at the University of Tennessee for stealing a basketball player's laptop. After a long and hard journey, Cameron Clear was back and playing in the Big Room.

The Aggies kicked off and Alabama's Chris Jones made a bad decision to run the ball back, and then made another dubious choice by running in a different direction from the blocking wedge set up in front of him. He was tackled at the Alabama eleven-yard line. The two-time defending national champions were showing signs of early stage fright. On consecutive plays, two Alabama lineman jumped the gun, while on the sideline, Nick Saban grimaced like a man who had just swallowed a spoiled oyster.

Alabama punted, and the Aggies took the ball back not far from midfield. Manziel the maestro was at top form. He moved his team downfield with almost ridiculous ease. Malena carried the ball from the one-yard line and stretched just enough to reach the goal line. The first quarter was not even half over, the Aggies were ahead 14–0, the ground seemed to vibrate while the fans rejoiced, and Alabama was, in the parlance of a Dixieland sheriff, "in a heap a trouble."

Though the game had barely started, the Tide offense faced a crucial series. Another three-and-out, and the defense, already winded and more than a little bit stunned by Manziel, would have to return to the field, and that prospect might mean that the national champs would be down 21–0. Against Manziel, that meant it would be time for last rites. Alabama play callers would have a treat the next drive as if it were the last one of the game.

A. J. McCarron was up to the task. After an incompletion, he hit a receiver for twelve yards. Alabama had picked up a first down—a small thing perhaps, but from the Crimson Tide perspective, it was like a cheeseburger to a starving man. McCarron then connected on a sequence of quick sideline passes that were just long enough to move the chains three more times. Then, from the twenty-two, McCarron delivered a kill shot. He hit Kevin Norwood at the junction of the sideline and goal line, and even though Norwood was tightly covered, he made a marvelous over the back-shoulder grab for the TD.

More bad news awaited the Aggies on the kickoff when return man Brandon Williams fumbled a bouncing squib kick out of bounds, and A&M took over at its own two-yard line. Manziel, though, was conspicuously untroubled. With his customary dispatch, he moved his team away from his own goal line, then across midfield. 'Bama's defensive adjustments had been deployed.

The Tide lined up with four down linemen, six defensive backs, and one other player whose assignment was to shadow Manziel. It didn't seem to be doing much good.

Then, a crucial play in the game happened. An apparent pass completion from Manziel to the amazing Evans inside the 'Bama ten-yard line was nullified. An official ruled that Evans had pushed off his defender, a fifteen-yard penalty. After an offsides call, the Aggies would be confronted with a third and thirty-one situation, which was a task that even Manziel couldn't master. The Aggies resorted to a tactic known as the punt, and during much of the Manziel era, many Aggies fans were not sure exactly what that was.

As the second quarter started, McCarron was getting into a solid rhythm. He advanced his team to the Texas A&M forty-four. Then, like Wee Willie Keeler at bat, he surveyed the A&M alignment and noted that centerfield was vacant. In other words, the Aggies positioned all of their defensive backs to the sidelines, which had been his basic point of attack.

McCarron called a flea-flicker play, handing off the ball to a running back, who quickly lateralled it back to the quarterback. The ploy froze the defensive back just long enough to allow his man to race past him and be suddenly alone in the unprotected middle of the field. That play has been used in football since Knute Rockne was a pup, and to this day, nobody has adequately explained the reason why it is known as flea flicker. It worked, and DeAndrew White was six yards behind his defender when he caught the football for an easy TD.

What had seemed a potential blowout not much earlier was then a tied game, 14–14, and as the Alabama fight song resounded throughout Kyle Field, the Aggies, football team and fans alike, realized that for the remainder of the afternoon, they would be experiencing what would amount to a two-and-half-hour roller-coaster ride.

On the next drive, the Aggies were moving again. They had advanced to point inside the Tide forty when Manziel faced a third-and-eight predicament. Third and thirty-one might not be consistently doable for Johnny Football, but third and eight was. However, just after taking the snap, Manziel ran to his left and straight into a major problem. Alabama defensive end Jeoffrey Pagan, constructed with same basic contours as a John Deere tractor, was unblocked and positioned to squash Manziel like a gnat on a windshield. Manziel, sensing sudden death, spun and retreated. But Pagan rumbled along in pursuit and suddenly had Johnny's maroon jersey wrapped in his huge fist. The referee had his whistle in his mouth, about to rule Manziel in-the-grasp and therefore down, but somehow, some way, the quarterback spun loose and continued his escape route, even though it was in the direction of his own goal line. Then a posse of five Alabama defenders joined the chase, and just before capturing outlaw Johnny thirty yards behind the line of scrimmage, he flung the football far downfield and miraculously into the hands of a leaping receiver, Aggie freshman Edward Pope, who caught it for the first down.

Of all of the superhuman stunts Manziel had performed in his Aggie career, that one would trump them all. They used to wrap Harry Houdini in chains, lock him in a safe, and throw him off the Brooklyn Bridge, and he'd pop back up the surface of the river in good health. But Harry Houdini on his best day had never pulled off an escape stunt like Manziel's. And he had pulled it off not against a bunch of Sam Houston State Bearkats, but the Alabama defense, the biggest and baddest in the whole damn country. Every person in Kyle Field wondered the same thing. How had Manziel done that? It couldn't have been real. He must have been using trick mirrors or something.

Curiously, however, Manziel was about to do something that was a serious departure from his magic show repertoire. At the Alabama goal line, with the Aggies poised to regain the lead, Mike Evans, Manziel's usual target, lined up to the right. Manziel instead threw the ball to the left, misfired, and the player who caught the ball, wide open in the end zone, was Cyrus Jones, conspicuously clad in a white jersey with crimson numerals.

Yikes. 'Bama got the football back via the end zone interception touchback and suddenly the ebb and flow of the epic contest was drifting clearly in Alabama's direction. It did not take long for McCarron to more fully seize the momentum. From one yard on Alabama's side of midfield, he threw a quick sideline pass to Kenny Bell, who had been single covered. The Aggie defender waved and missed—*ole!*—and Bell sprinted untouched the rest of the way for the touchdown.

'Bama could smell the blood. They scored yet another touchdown on a short run by T. J. Yeldon and led at halftime, 28–14.

In the third quarter, more adversity awaited the Aggies. Manziel had initiated a promising drive when a pass thrown into the center of the field bounced off the fingertips of the intended receiver and into the hands of Tide defensive back Vinnie Sunseri, who started back the other way. Manziel himself attempted to make the tackle on the interception return and it looked amazingly like one of the hundreds defenders had made seem so ridiculous during his own patented thrill-runs. Manziel dived at the ball carrier, missed him by five yards, and ignominiously fell on his ass. Sunseri continued to weave and dodge his way downfield and registered a seventy-three-yard touchdown return.

Texas A&M was down 35–14. If anybody could bring them back from that abyss, it was you-know-who. Had the Aggies been playing anybody but Alabama, he might have done it, too.

Manziel cranked out a touchdown pass to narrow the deficit to two touchdowns, and then Yeldon lost a fumble at the Aggies' five. On the next play, Manziel hooked up with Evans and the result was a ninety-five-yard scoring drive that took just one play. The Aggies appeared to be mounting a comeback of biblical proportions. But A. J. McCarron, experiencing the game of his collegiate career, would simply have no part of the comeback. He just would not have it.

Try as they valiantly did, A&M's defense could not stop Alabama. When the Tide scored its forty-ninth point, to take yet another two-touchdown lead, only 2:28 was left in the game. Manziel wasn't quite finished, and with fifteen seconds remaining on the clock, he threw his fifth touchdown pass of the game. Alabama recovered the onside kick attempt.

The Tide had won the game of the year, 49–42.

When McCarron dropped down on one knee to officially end the game, "[a] crowd of 87,596 that was booming like a jet engine earlier fell silent." That was how the Associate Press reported the scene.

Afterward, coaches and players seemed drained. Nick Saban was not overjoyed, but simply relieved, like a man who had just avoided a prison sentence. He did not have much to say: "I knew that we were going to have to play this way on offense to have a chance. I did not think [the Aggies] would score forty-two points, but they did."

What had saved Alabama had been its unorthodox four-one-six defense, employed after the Aggies had scored with ridiculous ease on their first two drives. That tactic had been a notable departure from conventional Tide defensive philosophy, which was trade-marked by a pursue-and-kill technique. At College Station, the plan had become to initiate a containment, damage-control tactic against Johnny, and it worked just enough, just barely. At the end, it probably could have been said that Nick Saban's staff had out-strat-egized Kevin Sumlin's on both sides of the ball. They had won the so called behind-the-scenes chess match. It wasn't as brain-busting as chess, of course, but more like tic-tac-toe since Xs and Os were being used.

In any event, after the game Kevin Sumlin seemed calm, almost serene. He called Manziel's performance "Johnny-like." Anybody who has ever seen him play knows that's about right.

Manziel was obviously subdued. He offered the glass-half-full outlook: "Well, this was not the Super Bowl game. Alabama lost a game last year and still won the national championship. Our season is not over."

So the Great Crash at College Station had finally ended. Fans of both teams felt wrung out and wilted as they departed the stadium.

Everybody needed a drink. Unlike the train wreck, nobody had been scalded or wounded by flying metal. But like the people who were there at Crush, Texas, in 1896, they realized they had witnessed something to be talked about for the rest of their lives.

12

THE REBOUND

VIRTUALLY ALL OF THE Texas-based sports commentators deemed the Texas Aggie exhibition against the Crimson Tide a moral victory. That was even more galling than a consolation prize that included a twenty-dollar gift certificate redeemable at most Walmart locations. Hell, moral victory? We were talking about a probable trip to the national championship game, and moral victories held no value in those circumstances. Even an immoral victory was better than that.

Columnists would further assert that while the Aggies had lost a 49–42 barnburner, they had demonstrated their mettle and proven that they could compete on the field against the top elements of the almighty football SEC. They seemed to forget that the Aggies had already accomplished that the previous season.

Johnny Manziel had duly noted that the Texas A&M season was not over. The remaining scheduled involved a list of foes that included the following: SMU, home game; Arkansas, at Fayetteville, the first road game of the season; Ole Miss, at Oxford; Auburn, home game; Mississippi State, home game; Vanderbilt, home game; UT–El Paso, home game; LSU, at Baton Rouge; and finally, Missouri, at Columbia.

A couple of off-weeks were conveniently placed in that autumn slate. From the vantage point of mid-September 2013, the prospect of running that table did not seem too far out of reach. SMU and New Mexico amounted to a couple of nonconference strolls though the tulip garden, in which Matt Joeckel and Kenny Hill— Johnny Football's potential successors as quarterback, presuming that he was to leave College Station and register for enlistment with the pros at the end of the season—would get ample playing time in the second half.

The trip to Fayetteville the following week had the potential to present some difficulty. The Hogs were working under a new coach, brought down from Wisconsin, and they would be improved, but only because they couldn't have been any worse than their horrid 2012 showing. The next game, at Ole Miss, would present a more significant challenge. Oxford was a potential death trap, as the Aggies had learned the year before, when they had staged a mad rally to snatch a comeback win there.

Then came a stretch of home games. Auburn and Mississippi State had been what amounted to fine dining for the Aggies 2012, and both of those runaways had happened on the road. Manziel had fine-tuned his Heisman Trophy credentials against that hapless duo, and would doubtlessly do so again. So the Tigers and the Bulldogs were slotted into the win category. Vanderbilt—well anyplace that called itself the Harvard of the South—would be in for a rude learning experience at a place like College Station, Texas. The visitors from Nashville had shed their doormat status under its up-and-coming coach James Franklin, but Vandy was still Vandy. Enough said there.

The challenge was the LSU assignment, over in Baton Rouge, where black magic ruled the atmosphere at Tigers Stadium. Les Miles' team seemed to be down a notch, though, and had not looked to be up its usual standards in early-season games. So LSU at Baton Rouge actually loomed as the kind of challenge that extracted the best from Johnny Football. That last game at Missouri could not be taken entirely for granted—this team seemed improved from the one that the Aggies had steamrolled at College Station in 2012.

So, if Manziel and friends could sweep the slate, and the odds seemed favorable that they might, the end of the season might indeed prove very interesting. 'Bama would need to lose two games for A&M to gain a slot in the SEC championship game at the Georgia Dome. The likelihood of 'Bama even being hard-pressed in one game seemed remote, much less two. But, stranger things had occurred, although nobody could remember when. Maybe A. J. McCarron would elope with Katherine Webb at mid-season and the couple would then run away to live forever in the south of France. If McCarron had been Brent Musburger, that's what he would have done. Or maybe the entire Tide team would be stricken by an epidemic of bird flu and forfeit its remaining schedule. Even if the Tide did not falter, the Aggies, if they did their job, would still wind up in a top BCS bowl and the fans could travel to a swell holiday football feast in someplace like Miami or New Orleans. They surely did not want to go back to the AT&T Cotton Bowl in Arlington.

Also in question was Johnny Football's prospect of repeating as the Heisman Trophy winner. His turbulent 2013 offseason had certainly not been helpful for building his case for reelection. That trophy was supposed to won on the playing field making touch-downs and not lost in hotel rooms autographing souvenir football helmets. But Heisman voters were media people in the whole and therefore prone to mood swings.

His primary competition would be McCarron. A. J. had not necessarily outplayed Manziel in the big game of the past weekend, but he had been awfully good. The knock against McCarron was that he was part of an eleven-man show and not the kind of one-man-band that wins the big postseason trophies.

Another contender for the prize was a quarterback that the pro scouts seemed to like better than Manziel. He was Teddy Bridgewater at Louisville. Bridgewater's big problem was, well, Louisville. The Cardinals were a Division I team, of course, and had beaten some big-reputation opponents. But Johnny Unitas had played at Louisville, and he sure as hell never won a Heisman Trophy. At end of the day, to utilize an overworked term, the University of Louisville was a basketball school and always would be.

One more personality, previously unknown, was making some early-season college football headlines. He was a freshman, but Johnny Football had shown that freshmen could win the Heisman Trophy. He played at Florida State, which was moving quickly upward in the college rankings, and his name was Jameis Winston. He had been accumulating some serious statistics while the Seminoles, under coach Jimbo Fisher, were chalking up impressive scores. Winston was a big son of a gun, and in the springtime, he threw ninety-five-mile-an-hour fastballs from a pitcher's mound and had already been drafted by the Texas Rangers.

So, much of the football talk on the A&M campus was focused on the future. The present, however, provided some attention as well, and it was comforting. It did not involve the Aggies, either, but rather the Texas Longhorns. Supporters of those two rivals—Longhorns and Aggies—loved it when the other team encountered misfortune. They didn't say so publicly, but they did. It was fun to watch the hated foe get beat, and when that happened, A&M and UT fans would obtain the kind of mean-spirited satisfaction that someone might feel after a bitter divorce when they learn that their ex-spouse has been pulled in for DUI.

What had been happening in Austin in the early games of the 2013 season was, from the Texas A&M point of view, all too rich.

After its loss in the BCS title game against Alabama that followed after the 2009 season, the Longhorns, under coach Mack Brown, had been wandering through the football wilderness in a daze. After that game, Brown privately told his friends that if Colt McCoy had not gotten injured early, UT would have won by three touchdowns. The disappointment had left Mack in a funk that he couldn't shake.

The following season had produced a losing team. The next two had finished 8–4, and any season that did not register at least ten wins at UT was deemed a flop. Even worse was that during the 8–4 campaigns, the headline event of the Longhorns schedule was the Oklahoma game at Dallas, and the last two of those had been disastrous, as the Sooners piled up more than sixty points in both contests.

The Orangebloods, as the fans were known, had been becoming more and more impatient with Mack Brown, a well-known figure on the sidelines since the 1998 season, when Ricky Williams had won the Heisman Trophy. Brown's tenure since had experienced some highs and lows. But after the one big high—the national championship win over USC after the '05 season, a contest that announcer Keith Jackson proclaimed to have been "the greatest game in the history of football"—it seemed that Mack Brown had forged a happy home that would endure a lifetime.

Austin, Texas, enjoyed a reputation as the coolest city in Texas. Well, if one thought that overwhelming all-day traffic jams were cool, that having a road system apparently designed by leading members of the local population of acid casualties was cool, that mountain cedar pollen that hung in the air like smoke and made everybody drown in their own snot was cool, that drought and insufferable heat was cool, that people shopping at the grocery store wearing bath robes was cool, then Austin deserved that designation. What had not been cool in recent years had been the football program, and nobody disputed that.

Mack Brown no longer seemed all that cool, either. He was over sixty years old, and had entered that plateau of life in which a man is too old to cut the mustard but can still lick the jar. His team had jumped the track and he didn't seem to have any idea how to get it back on. Recruiting had slipped, too. Brown's latest crop included just fifteen freshman candidates. Furthermore, in a time when quarterbacks were a prime ingredient in the modern, fast-tempo, no-huddle, spread offensive jamboree that the college game had become, Brown had badly misjudged the ones that he had brought in. Those included not one, but two guys with the first name of Connor. Everybody knows that football is no sport for a Connor.

Kids named Connor play soccer at all-white private high schools. Connor plays the bassoon in the youth orchestra. Connor enjoys baking little gingerbread men. Connor gets bullied on Facebook. Neither of Mack Brown's Connors would play a down at Texas, even with modest competition. The guy he had, David Ash, was no great shakes, either—not when compared to Manziel or, for that matter, hardly anybody else. His backup, Case McCoy, younger brother of Colt, probably could not have started for Sam Houston State.

In the early months following the 2012 season, it would be revealed that two high-powered figures in the money-and-politics element that actually ruled UT athletics had been working backstage in an effort to do Mack Brown in. It was a plot that carried conspiratorial overtones. Tom Hicks of Dallas, former owner the Texas Rangers and Dallas Stars and a man who had been instrumental in bringing Brown to Texas from North Carolina in the first place, and Board of Regents member Wallace Hall, also of Dallas, had covertly contacted Nick Saban's agent, Jimmy Sexton, also of Dallas, to see if Saban might be interested in leaving Alabama in favor of Austin if, of course, the price was right.

Brown was steadfast in his desire to remain on as the Longhorns head coach. At the conclusion of preseason workouts in 2013, while the Aggies were enduring the Johnny Manziel–NCAA ordeal, Mack Brown, via the media, had been assuring the Longhorns' huge fan base that the program had been fixed.

He loved, he said, what he witnessed in the drills. The roster was experienced and very athletic. The team, in 2013, would contend for national honors, like back during the not-so-far away good old days, Brown predicted. That boast, even if it came to pass, was unwise. Talk was cheap, and Brown should have fully realized that his team would have to do all of the talking in the form of wins on the field.

On the last day of August, when Manziel had been making his celebrated second-half grand entry against Rice, UT would open its season later in the early evening against another Aggie team, those being the Aggies of New Mexico State from Las Cruces. Texas would win the game, 56–7. So all seemed right in Longhorn-land.

But wait. There were high school teams in Texas that could have beaten New Mexico State, 56–7. Even as a low-echelon team, that bunch was conspicuously bad. Fact was, with about five minutes left to play in the first half, New Mexico State was ahead 7–0. The Texas quarterback, Ash, whose reputation for erratic play had been well earned during two previous seasons, was off-key again and had thrown a couple of picks against the lowly New Mexicans. Even more alarming was the UT starting defense. They'd been stigmatized as a poor tackling team the year before, and they missed tackles time and again in the opener. The New Mexico State version of the Aggies had absolutely no depth, and eventually caved in, but the overall performance of what was supposed to have been a top national contender was, at best, worrisome.

Then the Longhorns would travel to Provo to play Brigham Young. The Longhorns were ranked No. 15 in the nation while the Cougars had lost its opener, 19–16, to a ho-hum Virginia team.

Texas' showing at BYU was nothing short of wholesale disaster. The defense, the one that Brown had assured fans would be a dominant force, was stunningly, jaw-droppingly nonexistent. The BYU quarterback, Taysom Hill, could not believe his good fortune. Before the night was finished—and it had been a late night because the game had been delayed by a lightning storm—Hill would rush for 259 yards and three touchdowns. The Cougars would gain 550 yards on the ground, a school record, and win the game 40–23. "We knew we could run on them," Hill said. "But we sure didn't expect to break the school record. Once we saw that they weren't about to stop the run, there was no need to get away from it. So we didn't."

Many more showings like that one, and Brigham Young fans could start calling their starting quarterback Taysom Football.

Mack Brown, always a master of understatement, said simply, "We didn't do our job as players or coaches."

Even worse was the fact that the BYU debacle was scheduled for several replays during the coming the week on the Longhorn Network. Good thing for athletic director DeLoss Dodds that his network had been direly pressed to locate any cable or satellite providers to carry the thing.

The first thing Brown did on Sunday morning after the team's return to Austin was fire his defensive coordinator, Manny Dias, and replace him with Glen Robinson, an ex-coach who had been doing TV commentary. Such a drastic staff change at that point of the season could not be defined as anything other than panic. The Texas faithful wished that Brown hadn't stopped with Dias and had fired himself as well.

That, he was not about to do. Mack Brown, with his once-great kingdom collapsing all around him, had entered a state of full denial. In the next game, at home against Ole Miss with 101,000 Orangebloods jammed into the stadium and watching in horror, the Rebels stampeded the Horns, 44–23.

Mack Brown was cooked. He was finished as head coach at Texas and was the only person who didn't seem to grasp that. Media talk shows made a hot topic of speculating the identity of the man who would replace him. One name being tossed out was Kevin Sumlin. Well, if that happened, the Aggies' bonfire tradition would have to have been reinstated—at Kevin Sumlin's house.

Back in College Station, all week long, the talk was more about the smoldering wreckage over in Austin, and not the Aggies' upcoming appointment against SMU.

If Johnny Manziel kept a special place in his heart for an opposing football team, the main candidate would have to have been the Mustangs from Southern Methodist. It had been on SMU's campus the previous season where Manziel would not only register his first college victory, but also plant the seeds that would blossom into his remarkable football career.

The most important aspect of that game had been the off-hand, post-game remark of Aggies receiver Uzoma Nwachukwu in which he had referred to his quarterback as Captain Amazing and, immortally, Johnny Football.

So it had been in Dallas that the brand had been established. That Johnny Football label would do more than help ignite the justifiable hype, and it would be an ingredient that would eventually bring a lot of serious money to Manziel's doorstep. The moment Johnny Football signed his first NFL contract, he would immediately begin endorsing everything from condoms to Cadillacs.

The 2013 early-season version of the Ponies was shaping up as everything the Aggies had hoped they would be—which was to say, not very good. They had been mediocre in their home opener against Texas Tech. The Red Raiders were coached by A&M's ex-offensive coordinator Kliff Kingsbury, who'd taken to wearing shades on the sideline. If Aggies thought that Johnny Football had gone Hollywood on them, they should have checked out Kliff. SMU lost to Tech, 41–23, and that had been expected.

What was not expected happened in SMU's next game. The Mustangs barely beat Montana State, 31–30, before a very SMU-like home crowd of 10,101. Not good.

SMU, at that point, was not much good at anything athletically, although the basketball team was about to become extremely competitive under coach Larry Brown. The school was, if news reports were to be believed, tops in the nation in one category: date rape. Maybe that was just a Dallas thing. An uptown microbrewery was marketing a pale ale that might have been patterned after the typical SMU coed. They called it Dallas Blonde and promoted the product with the slogan, "It Goes Down Easy."

A female SMU student had written an op-ed piece for the school newspaper, the *Daily Campus,* that suggested that if some of the girls had not been so inclined to get commode-hugging drunk at those frat parties, they might not be victimized quite so frequently. It was a carefully worded essay. From the reaction, however, one would have thought she had quoted the line from former candidate for Texas governor (and proud Aggie) Clayton Williams, when he had infamously said, "Bad weather is like rape. If it's inevitable, you might as well relax and enjoy it." Pity the coed editorial writer. Campus women's groups wanted to burn her at the stake.

This stuff was making headlines in the SMU paper, unfortunately, because the football team was not producing much that made for good copy.

The game at College Station went exactly according to pre-game expectations. Under Manziel, the Aggies, having dropped to No. 10 in the Associated Press rankings following the loss to Alabama, had been dominant from the beginning. Manziel's career-highlight film, which was already something that would require an intermission if it ever made the theaters, would have to include one or two entries from the SMU game. One of those involved what might be submitted as the greatest seven-yard touchdown in the history of the school, during which Manziel side-stepped one potential tackler and then hurdled another.

A&M had led 32–6 at the half and never looked back. Manziel produced his customary eye-popping stats. Even more comforting was the performance of the A&M defense. In their first three games, the Aggies had yielded an average of thirty-six points. The results against SMU had been far more encouraging. "We're a work in progress for sure," said defensive coordinator Mark Snyder. "But as long as I keep seeing improvement each week, we'll be fine."

The Aggies did display some things that indicated the team was something other than flawless. Kevin Sumlin was less than pleased that the team was flagged for thirteen penalties.

Another tacky concern: placekicker Taylor Bertolet missed an extra point in the first half, and following the Aggies' next TD, he missed again. So Sumlin replaced Bertolet with Josh Lambo on the next attempt and the holder, Drew Kaser, fumbled the snap.

Manziel directed a touchdown drive on the Aggies' first possession of the third quarter, and then was given the rest of the night
off. So he sat relaxing on the bench and enjoying a cup of Gatorade
or perhaps O'Doul's—America's best-selling nonalcoholic beer. The
final score was 42–13, although nobody who actually attended the
game probably knew it. After it was evident that Johnny Football
had retired for the evening, the stands began to empty.

Even though Manziel's evening on the field had been an abbrevi-
ated one, SMU coach June Jones had seen plenty. Jones, who could
pass for a Marine Corps general, said, "We tried a little of everything
defensively to try to slow [Manziel] down. He is an amazing player.
You blitz him, and he is accurate with the ball. You rush three and
he can scramble around and make it last forever. He is a great college
football player, and he is in the perfect system."

Toward the end of the season, SMU would play against another
quarterback who was targeted as somebody who might be selected
above Manziel in the upcoming NCAA draft. That was Blake Bortles,
equipped with a body and arm that was cut directly from the NFL
template, from Central Florida. SMU almost knocked off Central
Florida, which finished its season ranked close to the top ten and
stunned Baylor in the Fiesta Bowl.

Media people and others asked June Jones to compare Bortles, as
a pro prospect, with Johnny Manziel. Jones did know a thing or two
about the NFL. He had once been head coach of the Atlanta Falcons.
Jones offered a little of the old hem and haw, and offered praise to
Bortles, who had not had a particularly good game against SMU,
although the game had been played in an ice storm.

"But compared to Manziel?" declared Jones. "Listen. Nobody
compares to that guy. Any other questions?"

13

SEC: THE COMBAT ZONE

ACCORDING TO A BIOGRAPHY of Theodore Roosevelt, Teddy, during his presidency, would conduct a press conference almost daily. Then, at the close of the work day, it was his habit to invite a trio of reporters into the oval office, pull the cork out of the jug, and talk about what he really thought was happening in national or world affairs at the time. What Teddy told the reporters at the off-the-record happy hour was often in direct contradiction to whatever he had said for public print earlier in the day.

Thus has it always been, mostly, with public figures in their dealings with the media. It makes sense. All politicians regard the truth as something deadlier than a king cobra. What they say and do while off-camera offers a much more distinct picture of their more genuine feelings.

One good example took place in Austin in the early months of 1992. A reasonably unknown former governor of Arkansas, Bill

Clinton, was seeking the Democratic nomination for the U.S. presidency. After speaking at a fundraiser, Clinton was confronted by the then-governor of Texas, Ann Richards. No reporters, as far as Richards knew, were within listening distance.

"Bill," she said, "I've been hearing a lot of talk about your womanizing, and I want to know what you're going to do about that."

"Aw, Ann, that's just politics. A bunch of lies," Bill responded. "You, of all people, ought to realize that after all that stuff they said about you, about the drug use and all that."

"They weren't lying about me, Bill," Richards said, "and they're not lying about you either."

The concept of being less than upfront with the news media has certainly long been the stock and trade of college football coaches. When it comes to playing politics, people running for public office could learn a thing or three from the ranks of the coaching profession. A bunch of years back, a coach at a Southwest Conference school was meeting a room full of media people and providing an analysis of his team for the upcoming season.

"And Birdwell from Mineral Wells gives us some much-needed depth in the defensive secondary," the coach said. Hours later, in a hospitality suite set up for the media, the coach was chatting with the only reporter left in the room, somebody who was one of those guys the coach thought he could trust, like Teddy's Roosevelt's cronies. The coach was buoyed by the effects of the truth serum that's contained in a bottle of Old Charter. He brought up the topic of a player he had mentioned earlier. "Birdwell," he said, "is the sorriest son of a bitch I have ever known in my entire life. He's got this rich uncle who donates a ton of the money to the school, so not only did I have to waste a scholarship on the bastard, I have to find a way to get him on the field for three or so minutes every game. I keep hoping somebody breaks his damn back."

An article in the sports section the next day noted that Birdwell (not the player's actual name) not only provided much-needed depth, but that his work ethic was an inspiration to the entire team.

So what the reporter (somebody this author happens to know pretty well, since it was him) was reporting was absolute horseshit, but at some psychological level, the reporter didn't actually realize it. And that condition did and still does prevail among the big majority of the members of the working press.

The self-serving jive being delivered by coaches and players in all sports in the current news climate is more pronounced than ever. That is because, in the minds of the media, what an athlete says (or tweets) is what makes the headlines, and not what he or she did in the actual game.

Kevin Sumlin, addressing the media at mid-week before the trip to Fayetteville to play Arkansas, told reporters that his team was in for a tough battle, that the Razorbacks were especially dangerous when playing at home because they have such enthusiastic fans. What Sumlin was actually thinking was something entirely different: "We're going to beat those guys. They lost to Rutgers last week, for Chrissake. But that crowd is going to make it harder than it ought to be. It's a night game, so they'll all be totally wasted. Just last week, an eighteen-year-old girl from Arkansas wrote a letter to Dear Abby. She said she was still a virgin and wondered if her brothers were gay. Those inbred maniacs scare the living crap out of me."

Arkansas fans—with their wonderful cheer "Woooooo Pig! Sooey!"—have been known to be some the most rabid in all of college sports. They take genuine pride, that's the only word for it, in who they are, which is a characteristic everywhere among people who are backwoods and broke. Often, they substantiate the stereotype. A friend once told me that he had been in the army with a soldier who had grown up outside the town of Mountain Home, Arkansas. "First day of boot camp," he recalled, "they were handing out toothbrushes and the kid from Mountain Home looked at his and said, 'What in the hell is this thing?'"

Razorbacks fans, if they wanted to, could produce a chant that went "We're Number Three! We're Number Three!" because in terms of percentage of persons living beneath the poverty level, Arkansas ranks behind only West Virginia and Mississippi.

Those Alabama Roll Tide people in their RV caravans dread their every-other-year excursion to Arkansas because the stretch of highway along Interstate 40 between Memphis and Little Rock is nothing more than a semi-paved nightmare. The American Automobile Association encourages drivers to avoid that route if possible. It has been under construction since the dawn of mankind, allegedly because somebody from Oklahoma stole the steam shovel. The bridge that crosses the White River is perpetually narrowed to one lane, and that lane is often shut down, too. Travelers sit for hours and watch the helicopters fly in and out, MedFlighting whatever is left of the people who have been rear-ended by eighteen-wheelers.

People who live in that region get by only by being imbued with a tough sense of pragmatism. That is well illustrated by the statement from one man, a native of the deep Ozarks, who had incurred the disfavor of a social worker. He had refused to involve himself in her efforts to have his son paroled from prison.

"Don't you love your son?" she begged.

"Yes," he said. "I love my son the same way I love the Korean War, as being something terrible that I somehow managed to survive."

Visitors to the state had better come prepared, because they are in for a hard time. Sumlin, for sure, knew what his team might encounter. What he did not want, at any point in the game, was for his team to fall behind. In an environment like Fayetteville, when the crowd has reason to go into a frenzy, the fortunes of the road team can go from bad to worse, and then everything falls apart.

So, when Texas A&M won the pre-game coin toss, rather than defer its choice to the second half, which has become the customary tactic in college football, the Aggies elected to receive the kickoff. It made perfect sense. In the seventeen previous games with Johnny Manziel as quarterback, the Aggies had scored a touchdown on its first possession thirteen times. The message was simple: we want to score first and, in the process, stop Arkansas' upset bid before it gets started.

On the very first play from scrimmage, the Aggies went for the knockout punch. Johnny Manziel took the snap, retreated with the seven-step drop that pro scouts insisted that he master, and threw the ball deep in the direction of Mike Evans, who was running a post pattern. Evans was covered by two backs. Arkansas was well-coached. The man the school had hired to resurrect the program, Bret Bielema, was like Brian Kelly at Notre Dame. He was old-school, detail oriented, and his teams were always—always—well prepared.

But even though the receiver Evans was well defended, Manziel threw an absolutely perfect pass that went for a forty-nine-yard gain on the first play of the game. The cry from the grandstand went from "Wooooo Pig!" to "Ohhhhhh Shit!"

The Aggies used Ben Malena for a few plays to bang the ball closer to the goal line, but the Razorbacks responded and Manziel found himself looking at a third-down crisis from the nine-yard line. Arkansas' defense was cocked and loaded. It stormed past the Aggie blockers as Manziel retreated to pass. The quarterback sprinted to his right. Mike Evans had run a pattern to the back of the end zone but turned and came back the other way. Evans and Manziel had developed a sense of timing and field position that amounted to mental telepathy. Manziel, who was about to be chased out of bounds, passed the ball at the last instant, directly to the exact spot where he knew Evans would be, even on a busted pattern. Bingo. Touchdown.

Arkansas was anything but through. As Sumlin had suspected, the red-clad Pigs would locate the soft spots in the Aggies' defense. If Sam Houston State could do it, so could the Razorbacks. And they did. The Aggies were ahead at the half, but only by a margin of 24–20.

In the final two quarters, Kevin Sumlin's game plan was based on playing the sure thing, controlling the ball, and avoiding turnovers. Also, when on the road in a close game, the best strategy involves running the clock, and that was what the Aggies did. In the second half, on thirty-six offensive snaps, the Aggies ran the ball twenty-nine times and passed it only seven. So Texas A&M would eventually win the game 45–33 in a classic demonstration of the favored road team, as the coaches all love to say, taking care of business.

Bret Bielema, whose Wisconsin teams had always been among the very best in the Big Ten and who had coached those teams into a Rose Bowl trip, had nothing but praise for his own team's performance and was impressed, but not surprised, by what the Aggies had to offer.

"Because of their quarterback, devising a game plan to try to stop that offense was the toughest challenge I've had in my entire coaching career," Bielema said in one of those rare moments when a coach has looked the assembled news media straight in the eye and told the truth.

Meanwhile, at Arkansas, the Aggies had set a school record by scoring forty or more points in eight straight games. The previous record had been three.

So the Aggies got on their chartered jet for the late flight back home from the primeval Ozarks in a mood that was not exhilaration but more than a sense of whatever satisfaction that is to be derived from the completion of an honest day's work. Even that wouldn't last more than twenty-four hours, because they realized another road trip awaited them on the following weekend—one that was fraught with more potential treacheries than the mission at Fayetteville.

Next was a return visit to Oxford to play Ole Miss, site of a near loss in 2012. Manziel had staged what could have been termed a miracle comeback, although that was at a point before the coaches had learned that their quarterback was one of those rare people who know how to breathe life back into a corpse. This next assignment would not be easy, a task akin to robbing the same bank twice. The team that awaited them at Ole Miss would be an improved version of what they had faced the previous season.

The Aggies' enjoyment of watching somebody make mincemeat out of the Texas Longhorns in Austin a couple of weeks earlier had been tempered by the fact that the "somebody" was a team A&M would soon have to play. Prior to the season, an analyst had examined the Aggies' schedule and divided the competition into three tiers: cupcake, average, and elite. The Arkansas Razorbacks actually qualified somewhere between cupcake and average. Ole Miss was up at the next level, between average and elite.

The Aggies still had ambitions of completing the rest of their schedule without a loss. Sumlin might best have taken the view espoused by the good people of Alcoholics Anonymous. First, he had to concede to the presence of a higher power (Alabama) and then to the approach of getting it done one game at time. It was a simple, two-step program. Sumlin didn't have time to get involved with the other ten steps, like taking a moral inventory or apologizing to all the people whose lives he'd helped to fuck up. Maybe Johnny Football could do that for him.

Of course, another trip to Oxford reinforced what a great idea it had been for Texas A&M to leave the Big 12 and join the SEC. Oxford still exuded a sense of quaint southern charm and was a vastly superior football weekend destination than shitholes like Waco and Stillwater. Those Ole Miss people—it was a rare treat just listening to them talk.

Author Bill Bryson captured the lexicon while recounting a trip to Oxford where he sought directions from a local woman in hopes of finding the old home of author William Faulkner.

> "You pocked on the skwaya?"
>
> "Yes."
>
> "Okay, honey, you git in yo' car and you makes the skwaya. You goes out the other end, twoads the university, goes three blocks, turns rat at the traffic lats, goes down the hill there, you un'stan'?"
>
> "No."
>
> "Hit doan really matter cuz hits closed now. You can look around the grounz if you woan, but you cain't go insod."

At Oxford, the visiting Aggies would have plenty to listen to, and once again, plenty to look at as well. All of the girls on the

Ole Miss campus looked exactly like A. J. McCarron's girlfriend. The setting was a little different from the weekend before in Fayetteville in that after the game, you didn't want to go home. Not right away, anyhow.

The Rebels, at game time, were playing at a level that was closer to average than elite. After beating Texas, they had experienced their first loss, to Alabama, and had actually been shut out, 25–0. That had been followed up by a 30–20 defeat to Auburn, which had apparently returned to the land of the living. Still, under coach Hugh Freeze, the Rebels were dangerous. Freeze was an intriguing kind of man. As a high school coach at Briarcrest Christian School in Memphis, he convinced the school to enroll a troubled kid named Michael Oher, who went on to the NFL. Oher was the topic of a book, and then a movie, called *The Blind Side*, and the story was so inspirational that the film, which starred Sandra Bullock and Tim McGraw, became the highest-grossing football movie ever produced. In the movie, Freeze's character, played by Ray McKinnon, was known as Coach Burt Cotton, but it had been the real-life Hugh Freeze who had provided the foundation for the actual narrative.

Perhaps a movie on the life story of Hugh Freeze might be in order. Here he was, coach of a grand old program in the nation's best football conference. As recently as 2009, though, Freeze had been coaching at someplace called Lambuth University in Jackson, Tennessee. A restaurant in Jackson called Suede, which contains displays of Carl Perkins memorabilia, was a lot better known in the town than the Lambuth Eagles football program.

In 2009, Freeze coached the Eagles to an unbeaten season that included wins over Kentucky Christian, Campbellsville, Bellhaven, and Shorter University. (Ever heard of Shorter? Me neither.) With Vaught-Hemingway Stadium jammed to the gills for a game that was nationally televised on ESPN against the ninth-ranked team in the United States, Hugh Freeze had come a very long way in a very short time.

For the fifteenth time in his eighteen career college games, Manziel directed a touchdown drive on his opening possession. On the first play from scrimmage, against a defensive setup that included two players to shadow his every move, Manziel took the snap and ran directly up the middle of the field. His shadows waved bye-bye—Manziel dodged past them, somehow untouched—and gained eighteen yards.

Then, on third and seven from near midfield, where the Rebels were expecting a short pass, Manziel instead went deep and connected with Travis Labhart at the ten. A run by Malena got the TD, and once again, the Aggies had secured the early lead that was so vital to making a living on the road in the SEC.

But, as Sumlin and almost every player on the Aggies team had anticipated, the game soon developed into a back-and-forth thrill show in which it was obvious that the team that had the ball last would be the winner. The Ole Miss quarterback, Bo Wallace, was not timid about sharing the stage and swapping touchdowns with Manziel. Texas coach Mack Brown had attempted to recruit Wallace out of junior college and almost succeeded. If he had, Wallace might well have saved Brown's job.

With 6:08 left in the game, Wallace threw a fifty-yard touchdown pass to Jaylon Walton that put Ole Miss up 38–31. The game was eerily like the one the season before. But as Labhart, the Aggies receiver whose catch had set up A&M's first touchdown, said after the game, "When they [Ole Miss] hit that go-ahead touchdown, Johnny and I just looked at each other and laughed. Not because we thought Ole Miss was bad or anything. We just simply knew that we would come right back and score ourselves."

Which, of course, they did. On the game-tying drive, Manziel directed a ground assault, doing most of the running himself, including the six-yard run that tied the game at 38–38 with three minutes to play. The Aggies defense got the stop, so A&M would indeed be the last team to have the ball. Two runs by Manziel put the Aggies within easy reach of the field-goal kicker, Josh Lambo.

His thirty-three-yarder sailed between the uprights with 0:00 left on the clock.

Johnny Football and his receivers might have been laughing on the sideline when Ole Miss had taken its late lead. But Kevin Sumlin had not seen the humor in the situation.

"I hope that the person who makes up the SEC schedule does not mess up and send us to Oxford for the third straight year," he declared, "because I don't ever want to come back here again."

Once again, that rarest of rare events had taken place. A college football coach had told the truth.

14

HARD KNOCKS

THIS AUTHOR ATTENDED HIGH SCHOOL with a guy who had transferred in after flunking out of a rich kids' private school back East. "They gave me an IQ test back there," he said proudly, "and the score was so low, they couldn't believe it and made me take it again." Later in life, this same guy would change his name to Papa Pilgrim and ultimately die in an Alaskan penitentiary.

What a waste of a low IQ. What he should have done, immediately after not finishing high school, was become an expert analyst on a radio sports talk show. He could have even gone national like Mark Schlereth, an ex-jock who also had Alaska connections. In his in-depth preseason dissection of the teams in the NFC East, he went way out a dangerous limb and boldly predicted that the team that would be the division champion—and Schlereth said this on coast-to-coast ESPN radio—would be the "team that played the best." That was a daring declaration, one that female section editors at newspapers would term "ballsy." It turned out, though, that Schlereth was wrong. The team that eventually won that division, the Philadelphia Eagles, was not the team that played best, but rather, least bad.

Talk-show operatives share one universal characteristic, and that happens to be a highly truncated world view. It is as if all of these guys have been home-schooled by snow monkeys. Persons in this occupation really reach their full potential in cerebral, toe-to-toe debates, shouting matches really, on such issues of importance as, say, which quarterbacks deserve to be installed in the NFL Hall of Fame and which ones don't. It's too bad they only discuss sports, because otherwise listeners could treat themselves to Socratic discussions on all kinds of subjects.

Expert I: "You claim that Saturn is a greater planet than Jupiter?! Have you been tested for drugs lately?! Jupiter is at least twice as big as Saturn! It's the biggest planet in the entire . . . wudda-ya-call-it!"

Expert II: "Yeah. But Saturn has more rings."

Of course, a player like Johnny Manziel would be a topic for the leading minds within the higher counsels of the jock-world think tank. On the Saturday of the Aggies' win over Mississippi, the ex-coach Lou Holtz, a man who should have known better, sat in front of ESPN television cameras and asserted that A. J. McCarron was a better all-round quarterback than Manziel because Johnny Football made too many flashy plays.

As the 2013 season was reaching its midpoint, the college football battlefront was predictably unpredictable and providing rich and ample fodder for the sports radio combatants in the War of the Words. Before the season, coach Bob Stoops at Oklahoma had generated a media storm when he said that from top to bottom, the Big 12 was a tougher league than the SEC. Was he nuts? Perhaps not. Baylor, of all teams, under Art Briles, the coach instrumental to bringing Texas high school football out of its cave and into the modern age, was generating big interest. Those Bible-banging Bears had been beating some halfway decent teams by scores like ten thousand to 26. Stoops' Oklahoma team had put itself in the discussion as a possible candidate for a slot in the BCS Championship

Game. The Sooners, equipped with a big Tim Tebow–type quarterback named Blake Bell, a.k.a. the Belldozer, had gone to South Bend and pretty much pulverized the Notre Dame Fighting Irish.

The Oklahoma–Texas game, an annual highlight of the State Fair in Dallas, had once again worked out as a one-sided affair. The final score was 36–20, but that did not accurately reflect the dominance of the winning team that afternoon. The strange thing about the game was that the winning team was Texas. The Longhorns, heavy underdogs, had rocked the Sooners with two long touchdown passes, a TD punt return, and a thirty-yard TD interception return by a tackle. For one surreal afternoon, Texas' ability-challenged quarterback, Case McCoy, had played like Johnny Manziel, and Mack Brown had coached like Nick Saban. As it would turn out, that was indeed just for a day, but go figure. The day after the big upset, Kevin Sherrington of the *Dallas Morning News* wrote a column that begged Mack Brown to do the practical thing, the wise thing, and announce his retirement. Quit on the bright side. Brown was not about to take the advice, and he instead started issuing blather about trying to win the Big 12 championship.

Meanwhile, after two weeks on the road at Arkansas and Ole Miss, the Aggies were contentedly back home in College Station. The opponent was Auburn and the pre-game dynamic in College Station's Northridge saloons did not approach the feverish anticipation that had accompanied the Alabama game. To A&M fans, as the season rolled into its second half, the ground-shattering 'Bama game seemed like something that had occurred in the distant past, like the Crash at Crush.

The Aggies had been ascending since then in the AP poll one level a week, and with Auburn in town, they were resting at No. 7. Fans thought the Auburn game might be entertaining for maybe even two and a half quarters. The Tigers had lost every SEC game they had played in 2012, but the current edition was not half bad. Things were looking up under the new coach, Gus Malzahn. Some people speculated that he got the job because some Auburn people thought that Malzahn might have been distantly related to Manziel.

Not the case, obviously, but Auburn was clicking nicely under the guidance of Gene Chizik's replacement. LSU had beaten Auburn in September, but that had been the Tigers' only loss, and the team seemed to be improving with each game. It was broadly assumed that such progress would be stalled at College Station. Despite the fact that Auburn had cracked the AP top twenty-five, the Aggies had been posted as a solid twelve-point favorite.

Kyle Field was its usual sold-out self for the 2:30 p.m. kickoff. Autumn and football, the kind of setting that the old TCU coach Abe Martin had described as "Saturday's America," had embraced College Station. There are certain times of the year, like mid-October through mid-November and mid-April through mid-May, when Texas is a truly habitable place, and the game-time afternoon temperature at Kyle Field that day was a humane seventy-one degrees—over twenty degrees cooler than the day of the Alabama game.

Gus Malzahn liked that. Relieved of the prospect of having to endure sixty minutes of playing time in the convection oven that daylight affairs in Texas can become, Malzahn was pinning his hopes on the notion that if his team could somehow still be in the game at halftime, the Tigers might find a way to somehow wear the home team down in the second half. He'd put his Tigers through a hard-ass preseason, and this team, if nothing else, was extremely well conditioned. The problem would be living up to the first part: staying on the field with the perennially fast-start Aggie offense. As usual, the Manziel assault group came out firing full blast and gunning for a Mike Tyson-in-his-prime first-round knockout.

Mike Evans, A&M's ultra-talented pass catcher, had been shut down to a certain extent the week before at Ole Miss. Rebels coach Hugh Freeze had made a gamble by attempting to cover Evans with a six-foot-four freshman who had not previously even been on the field, and the freshman had done a phenomenal job.

Evans was dead set on redemption. Like Manziel, Evans had clear intentions of entering the NFL draft. The scouts were watching his every move, and off-games like the one at Oxford translated into a shrunken draft-day paycheck. So Mike Evans utilized the showcase of the Auburn game to produce one of the greatest games by a college pass receiver at anytime, anywhere.

At the end of the game, Evans had caught eleven Johnny Manziel passes for a total of 287 yards. That averaged out at twenty-six yards a catch. Among those catches were four that went for touchdowns of twenty-six, sixty-four, forty-two, and thirty-three yards. A great many of those 287 yards were accumulated after the catch. His performance was nothing short of breathtaking, and Mike Evans, for any pro scouts who might have been paying attention, put on a show that was worthy of the second coming of Calvin "Megatron" Johnson of the Detroit Lions.

Despite Mike Evans' amazing day, however, the Aggies were confronted by a team that was unexpectedly good. Yeah, A&M figured that Auburn might be pretty good, but had certainly not anticipated playing a team that was every bit as good as Alabama. The Tigers' Nick Marshall was a damn slick quarterback, and their running back, Tre Mason, was simply the best one the Aggies would face all season.

At the half, A&M led 24–17, but the Tigers were positioned just where Gus Malzahn had hoped they would be, which was still in the game. The Aggies continued to maintain their lead during the third quarter—Auburn still played tough, but there was no sensation of high anxiety in the huge crowd at College Station until about two minutes deep into the fourth quarter. Manziel made an eight-yard run and got knocked off his feet with one those "welcome to the SEC"–type tackles. Manziel attempted to jump back up, but couldn't. He lay back down on the field, and the Aggies' crowd issued a kind of gasp, like the one that goes out when the Olympic gold medal candidate figure skater slips and falls on her ass.

A&M trainers formed a circle around Manziel. After what seemed to be two of the longest minutes in the history of Kyle Field, Johnny Football finally stood up, but instead of returning to the offense, he walked off the field. There had probably been more laughter and good cheer about the airship Hindenburg when it blew up than there was at Kyle Field while the audience watched Manziel head unsteadily to the bench.

Matt Joeckel strapped on his helmet and entered the piercing glare of the spotlight. He'd felt that before in the first half of the Rice game, but he had the comfort then of knowing that Manziel would be out for the second half. Now Joeckel could not be sure whether the Heisman Trophy winner would return or not, and for all he knew at that moment, it might be his football game to win or lose.

The first play he ran as Manziel's emergency stand-in happened to be a third-down situation. Joeckel threw an incomplete pass and the Aggies punted. They still led the Tigers, 34–24, but Auburn, ferocious and determined, drove for a touchdown that cut the Aggies' lead to three points.

After the kickoff, it was Matt Joeckel, and not Johnny Manziel, who took the field to quarterback the Aggies. The crowd attempted, with limited success, to suppress its moans. Joeckel threw an interception. Attacking an SEC defense might not have been as easy as Manziel made it appear. It seems that all of those media cynics who had said the Aggies would be a losing team without Johnny Football just might have been right.

Auburn shoved the ball down the Aggies' throat and took the lead, 38–34. Gus Malzahn's pre-game strategy was working. The Tigers kicked off again. This time, Johnny Manziel came back onto the field, rejoicing cries resounded through the Lone Star State, and the torrential volume of calls to the College Stadium suicide-prevention hotline subsided. Johnny's right shoulder seemed to be bothering him, but not enough to prevent him from doing his usual thing. Batman had returned. Kapow. Aggies score. Aggies lead, 41–38.

The problem was that Gus Malzahn's team, in its way of thinking, hadn't traveled all the way to Texas for nothing. The Tigers' offensive line took a plant-the-flag-on-Iwo-Jima mentality and almost literally trampled the Texas A&M defense. They took back the lead, 45–41. Manziel needed to perform yet another miracle, something he was good at, but even Jesus Christ probably had more than one minute and seven seconds to turn the water into wine.

On the game's final play, Auburn defenders staged what looked like a buffalo stampede, and before Manziel could launch a pass somewhere roughly in the direction of Mike Evans, he got trampled.

Game over.

Mike Evans had played one of the most memorable games ever by a Texas Aggie football player, but in the end, the day would actually belong to Tre Mason, the Auburn running back, who had hammered the ramparts twenty-nine times and gained over 170 yards. "That is Auburn's identity," Mason said after the game as he blinked away genuine tears of joy. "Tough, hardnosed football. We're going to run the ball, and if you can't stop it . . . oh, well."

At the end of the season, Auburn would beat Alabama. If Aggies could have known that as they departed Kyle Field, they still would not have felt less sick. And nobody felt sicker than Mark Snyder, the Texas A&M defensive coach. "In my career," he said, "when you score forty-one points, you should win. End of story."

The following week, with UT El Paso at College Station, an odd scenario had crept in. The Aggies had lost two games by the span of a gnat's ass to what would turn out to be two of the best three teams in the United States. A&M actually should have beaten one, and certainly could have beaten the other. Yet, given the lofty expectations that greeted the 2013 campaign, at the halfway point the Aggies were looking at a season on the rocks.

The UTEP game was nothing more or less than a scheduling farce. When the school was still known as Texas Western, it had gained basketball immortality by upsetting the Kentucky Wildcats in one of the most acclaimed Final Four title games ever played.

A movie was made about that team. The college also produced Bob Beamon, who long-jumped over twenty-nine feet at the Mexico City Olympics in 1968 in the most stunning single event in the history of track and field. But the Miners' football highlights through the years could have been inscribed upon the head of a pin, and the 2013 edition really sucked. A&M won 57–7.

Nobody really knew what to expect next. Vanderbilt was clearly a football team that was going nowhere, although the week before they had upset the Georgia Bulldogs. But given the disappointment of having definitely been eliminated from contention to play for a national championship, might the Aggies collapse? That had happened to other teams throughout the years that had been just as good, just as proud as this one.

The degree of separation that exists between great teams and ones that are not very good can be lens-paper thin. Kevin Sumlin knew he would somehow have to continue to stoke his team with high levels of motivation. The losses to Alabama and Auburn had been disappointing. A loss to any of three teams coming up on the home schedule would be plain ugly. It was not unthinkable, though, and how badly hurt was Johnny Manziel?

Vanderbilt, despite its absolute lack of recent history as a football powerhouse, is an interesting school in an interesting city—Nashville. The college campus is located on West End Avenue, not awfully far from downtown and Union Station. Nearby is Nashville's historic First Baptist Church, which is across the street from a synagogue. In the 1930s, the church burned, and an agreement was reached for the churchgoers to temporarily conduct their services in the synagogue. One Sunday morning, a fully oiled wino watched the Baptists file into the temple, turned to a companion, and said, "Ya know, that's the shabbiest-lookin' bunch of Jews I ever saw."

Vandy, the so-called Harvard of the South, long ago fielded a good football team. (So did Harvard, for that matter.) The school provided cushy jobs to star football players, such as having to ride the streetcar all day to make sure that the conductor wasn't stealing nickels or working as a "greeter" at the Joy Florist shop. The greatest sportswriter of all time, Grantland Rice, went to Vanderbilt. On one occasion, Rice wrote a poem about the Vandy team that began, "Whenever we kick off against Tennessee, I open up a bottle of Hennessey."

None of these facts would be of much use to the gold-and-black Commodores at College Station. If Johnny Manziel was hurt, he didn't play like it. The Aggies breezed through, 56–24. Perhaps the experience of performing on the same field with Johnny Football inspired the Vandy team. After that, the Commodores went on the biggest winning spree in the modern football era of the school and defeated, in succession, Florida, Kentucky, Tennessee, Wake Forest, and finally the University of Houston in a bowl game. Vandy's coach, James Franklin, was rewarded with a job offer from Penn State, which he accepted.

Mississippi State was the next A&M opponent. This was the final home game of the year for the Aggies, and it was almost certain to be Johnny Football's farewell performance at Kyle Field. The Bulldogs came into College Station with modest credentials. They had won four games, but those had been against the likes of Alcorn State, Troy, Bowling Green, and Kentucky. The Aggies won the game, supplying some great moments in the process, and Manziel completed thirty of thirty-nine passes. But the overall result amounted to a dubious kind of masterpiece, like a painting done by Grandma Moses after she had arthritis so bad she could scarcely grip the brush. The final score was 51–41, and throughout the game, the Aggies' faithful maintained a chant directed at Manziel: "One more year! One more year!"

Hell. Why not two?

Next would be a trip to LSU to play the Tigers. Texas A&M still held hopes of finishing the season with a 10–2 record and maybe, just maybe, an invitation to one of those BCS bowl games that offered a whopper of a performance fee.

LSU had just gotten flattened by Alabama at Tuscaloosa, but facing the Tigers in that huge stadium of theirs on the banks of the mighty Mississippi River was always a daunting experience. Texans have traditionally counted on nasty receptions when they cross the state line into Louisiana bayou territory. Just look at what happened to Bonnie and Clyde.

Those LSU football fans are really a breed unto themselves, and anybody who ever plays at Baton Rouge can thank God for that. The tailgate scene is otherworldly. The natives love to cook up some traditional Cajun taste treats. Every recipe calls for two tablespoons apiece of cayenne pepper, paprika, and onion salt. What you'll find at many of the tailgate sites, roasting over hot and smoky coals, is a six-foot alligator stuffed with crawfish and Andouille sausage cornbread.

And, oh brother, these people could have taught Dean Martin a thing or two about getting drunk. When fans wander through the tailgate area clad in the colors of the visiting team, the LSU partiers drop everything, stare, point, and shout, "*Tig-uh bait! Tig-uh bait!*"

"The atmosphere isn't what I would call hostile," says an LSU grad. "But it's definitely what I would call . . . uh . . . competitive." LSU students have a knack for obtaining the cell phone numbers of big-time visiting quarterbacks and inundating the guys with threats and insults via text and voice message. Tim Tebow received stuff so vile it couldn't have been reprinted in *Hustler* magazine. Manziel would get the same treatment, but after the turbulent ride of his offseason, he was impervious to the poison darts of the haters.

Inside Tiger Stadium—a place where opponents' dreams go to die, as LSU coach Les Miles liked to say, and a place that they don't call Death Valley for nothing—Aggie fans awaiting the start of the game received a cheerful greeting from the LSU student section: "Go to hell, A&M, go to hell! Go to hell, A&M, eat shit! . . ." Then there was a serenade, sung to the melody of the old hit song "Hey Baby." It went: "H-e-e-e-y Aggie! I want to know right now if you'll be my bitch."

Sean Payton, the coach of the New Orleans Saints, was among the 92,949 people in the stands to watch the game and scout the quarterbacks. Payton was probably more interested in checking out LSU's Zach Mettenberger than Johnny Manziel, who would likely not be available to the Saints. Under Payton, New Orleans has always finished high and drafted low.

Ever since the Kevin Sumlin–Johnny Manziel show had opened back in September 2012, the Aggies had never lost a road game. It was not long into the contest at Baton Rouge that it became evident that run would be coming to a close. The Aggies never got started and the Tigers never got stopped. Manziel threw a fifty-one-yard touchdown pass to Derel Walker near the end of the first half—and then, as Porky Pig used to say, "Th-th-that's all, folks."

The ill-fated trip to Baton Rouge was not only Manziel's first road loss; it was also the first time he'd never really been in the game. He finished the night with only sixteen completions in forty-one attempts and the Aggies got beat, 34–10. His post-game comments were terse and to the point. "We got punched in the mouth and it wasn't fun. It wasn't fun tonight at all," he said.

One more regular-season game remained on the team's calendar, against Missouri on the road. Gary Pinkel's Missouri group had to be ranked neck-and-neck with Auburn as the SEC's surprise team of the year. A candidate for second division, the Tigers had lost only to South Carolina. The Aggies' only actual motivation at Columbia was that by winning, they could keep Mizzou out of the SEC championship game at Atlanta. But what the hell. Missouri was no grudge match. What had those guys ever done to the Aggies? They had never vandalized the Aggies team bus and loaded it with horse shit like Texas Tech had done in 2011.

So the Aggies were playing for cheap thrills and self-esteem. Missouri scored last on a long run from scrimmage in the fourth quarter and won the game, 28–21. Manziel played most of the game encased inside an invisible container of sheer hurt. In the second quarter, at the exact second Manziel was delivering a TD pass, he received an on-rushing helmet right square in the breastbone courtesy of Michael Sam, the SEC defensive player of the year. It was the hardest hit Manziel would sustain in his entire college career. Johnny Manziel's last regular-season possession ended with a three-and-out and that was that. Three of the Aggies' four losses had been against teams that called themselves the Tigers.

The game people actually cared about, one that probably got as high a TV rating in College Station as the Aggie–Missouri game, happened earlier in the day. That was the Alabama–Auburn game, the good old Iron Bowl. Just as they had in College Station, Auburn had trailed most the game before finally tying it, 31–31. But on the game's final play, the Tide had an opportunity to avoid overtime by making a long field goal, preserve its unbeaten record and season-long No. 1 ranking, and play yet again for another national championship, probably against Florida State.

Bang. The kick appeared to be good midflight, but it came down just short and fell into the hands of Auburn's Chris Davis, who was stationed as far back in the end zone as he could get. Davis took off. Alabama's field goal team, part of the best-coached team in the whole, wide universe, seemed to be somehow unaware that it was within the rules to run back a missed field goal. Nick Saban's players, most of them, sort of stood by like statues in the park while Davis raced along the sideline, and before they realized what was happening, the man was long gone.

Rod Bramblett, the Auburn radio play-by-play man, described the event: "The kick is on the way and . . . it's short! No good! Davis catches the football and runs it out the end zone. He's at the twenty, the twenty five, the thirty"—and here Bramblett's voice picked up cadence and intensity. "The thirty-five, the forty! The forty-five, the fifty . . . and Auburn's gonna win the football game! Auburn's gonna win the football game! Auburn's gonna win the football game!"

Bramblett sounded just like Russ Hodges calling the famous Bobby Thomson's home run—the shot heard 'round the world—in 1951. At that precise moment, everybody in America who was watching Chris Davis' feat wished that he or she was an Auburn fan.

Well, except for the Roll Tide people. They'd rather gargle weed killer than be Auburn fans. But for the time being, they just didn't want to be an Alabama fan.

15

ADIOS

DECEMBER ARRIVED, and Johnny Manziel and his Texas
Aggies compadres sat home in College Station to contemplate
the main events from the season-that-might-have-been as they
awaited their bowl game destination. There was a galaxy of possibilities there. Perhaps A&M might secure a berth in the Wilcox
Cremation Services Crystal Urn Bowl in Wiggin, Mississippi. Or
perhaps the Philips Milk of Magnesia Bowl in Compton, California,
or, with any real luck, the FeelGood Breast Augmentation Bowl in
Reno, Nevada.

OK. All right. Those bowls do not really exist. But the San Diego
County Credit Union Poinsettia Bowl does. So do the Famous
Idaho Potato Bowl in Boise and the Kraft Fight Hunger Bowl in San
Francisco. The final bowl matchups wouldn't be formally announced
until after the four postseason conference championship games
were completed, and those were scheduled on Pearl Harbor Day.
Auburn and Missouri would be the surprise guests at the SEC title
game in the Georgia Dome. Florida State and another dark horse,

Duke, would meet for the ACC championship game in Charlotte. It would be Ohio State versus Michigan State going for Big Ten honors, playing indoors in Indianapolis. At Sun Devils Stadium in Tempe, Arizona, Stanford had beaten out the Oregon Ducks to play Arizona State for the Pac 12 Territorial Trophy. From those eight teams, the BCS voters would select the two that would go at it for the national championship after New Year's in the Rose Bowl. Coaches hated playing those post–regular season, pre–bowl game extravaganzas, except for the coaches whose contracts provided incentive bonuses for appearing in one.

The month of December is the season for all of the big awards. Johnny Manziel would get blanked. The Pope would beat him out for the title of *Time* magazine's Person of the Year. *Sports Illustrated* would designate Peyton Manning as Sportsman of the Year, and the magazine's renowned cover curse would rise again to bite Manning in the neck at the Super Bowl. And Jameis Winston at Florida State replaced Manziel as winner of the Heisman Trophy in a landslide vote. A. J. McCarron finished second, but way back, and Manziel was fifth. For the second straight year, the award for the best college football player in America—the world, really, since the United States is the only country where the sport is seriously played by colleges—would be a freshman. At least Manziel could derive some satisfaction from serving as a Heisman Trophy trendsetter.

In a larger and, in the long run, much more important context, Johnny Football's 2013 season was anything but misspent. After the garish publicity that had accompanied the first eight months of the year, what mattered most was what would happen to Manziel off the field rather than on it. Everybody knew what he could do on the field; that much had been firmly established during his Heisman Trophy season and there was nothing he could have done to have improved on his reputation.

It had been the other stuff that the media and blog vultures had been anticipating—the wayward tweets, or perhaps some brand-new after-hours misadventure in a Northridge pub—that the

Sons of the First Amendment could magnify and exploit. Johnny had given them nothing. He seemed to have heeded the words Dr. Phil McGraw had spoken over the summer. Remember? Back when America's foremost on-the-air shrink (which he was, since Dr. Joyce Brothers had died on May 13) had observed it was the pro teams, and not necessarily the media, that Manziel should best make his object of concern. One more screwup might push him into the scruffy lower-income neighborhood that existed down there beneath the first round of the draft.

So Johnny Nightlife had morphed into Johnny Eagle Scout.

He had proven that he had developed a mature and practical sense of self-awareness. That was more than Mack Brown at the University of Texas could say. While the bowl game invitations were being dealt out, Brown had been the big story in postseason football throughout the state. The Longhorns had been routed at home by Oklahoma State late in the season and had collapsed in the second half of the final game at Baylor. The Texas players had barely gone through the motions in those games and offered a really impressive imitation of a team that did not give a damn.

Every follower of the UT program, from lukewarm to avid, wanted Brown gone, and it was obvious after the Baylor game that he would be. Well, obvious to everybody but Mack Brown. While his fiefdom was burning down all around him, Mack Brown kept babbling on about getting his team prepared to play Oregon in the friggin' Alamo Bowl. The president of the school, William Powers, and the new athletic director, Steve Patterson, had arranged a scenario that would enable Brown to exit gracefully. They issued a public statement indicating that Brown could stay on or retire—it would be up him.

Brown took on the role of the embattled and defiant man. He said the only place he intended on going anytime soon was on a recruiting trip to Florida. During this time, William Powers had been in a fight for his job as well, but Powers prevailed in a power struggle with the Board of Regents in a game of hardball politics.

Once his position was finally secure, he contacted Brown and said, "Uh, Coach, we need to talk." Only after that session did Brown, wearing the same grim look on his face that UT fans had come to know so well after countless (well, nine) bitter defeats at the hands of Oklahoma, confirmed he had "retired."

Names of his possible replacement wafted through Austin like that mountain cedar pollen in the springtime, and Nick Saban's was one of them. Finally, Steve Patterson settled on Charlie Strong of Louisville. However, had the Mack Brown replacement process not played out in the embarrassing, protracted, and sloppy mess that it had become, Nick Saban might very well have appeared at a press conference wearing a burnt-orange sweatshirt.

Another well-known coaching personality in Texas had experienced a year to forget as well. Gary Kubiak, head coach of the Houston Texans, had found himself stuck in the sausage-grinding machine that coaching becomes when things go bad. Kubiak, like Johnny Manziel, had once upon a time been a quarterback at Texas A&M. Since becoming head coach of the Texans, the lost-at-sea franchise that entered the NFL as an expansion team in 2002, Houston had finally developed as an up-and-coming contender in the AFC. Kubiak's team had won its division and one playoff game during the two previous seasons, and the fans who were filling Reliant Stadium, built not far from the old Astrodome, were expecting much more in 2013.

Instead, the Texans had somehow transformed themselves from up-and-coming to down-and-going. After winning their first two regular-season games, the canoe sprung a leak and then began to sink. Down, down, down. The fair-weather Houston fans were becoming surly. Houston pro football fans get that way; they have a right to be. Teams representing the city have never appeared in a Super Bowl. Jacksonville, Detroit, and Cleveland are the only other cities home to NFL teams that can match that claim. In the late 1970s, a man in Houston murdered his son during an argument over whether or not Earl Campbell should get a new contract. That event caused one columnist to opine, "They were probably the only two people in Houston who give a damn about the Oilers."

As the 2013 was going up in flames, some drunk fans located the home address of the quarterback, Matt Schaub. They went to his house, rang the front doorbell, and demanded an explanation for the team's poor showing. And when Schaub got hurt a week later, a large portion of the crowd at Reliant Stadium let out a lusty cheer. In early November, when the Texans were involved with yet another trying afternoon against the Indianapolis Colts, Gary Kubiak collapsed on the field while walking to the dressing room at halftime. He was placed on a stretcher and taken to a hospital. Nobody cheered, possibly because most of the fans had gone to the concession stands to buy more beer.

Kubiak remained hospitalized for a few days, and eventually, owner Bob McNair rewarded Kubiak for his travails by firing him. So after winning their first two games, the Texans lost their remaining fourteen, beating out the Washington Redskins for the top pick in the 2014 draft. Conspiracy theories drifted through humid streets of Houston and the NFL as a whole. Had the Texans tanked on purpose? Was it just possible that the Texans figured the franchise could reinvent itself via Johnny Football Fever?

Manziel had one final appearance set up in a Texas Aggies uniform. On New Year's Eve, the team would be in Atlanta to play Duke in the Chick-fil-A Bowl. Duke and Texas A&M were an odd sort of pairing. The school that would oppose A&M was named after Doris Duke, a jillionaire whose source of wealth was a Carolina tobacco fortune. Although the college enjoyed a wonderful academic reputation, it might be said that its main contribution to society was lung cancer.

The Blue Devils football team occupied a back seat to the basketball program—so far back that no one could see it. In a historical footnote, the 1942 Rose Bowl game was played in Durham, North Carolina. After the start of World War II, the national security people were fretful over the possibilities that a giant crowd on the West Coast might encourage a Japanese attack, so the Blue Devils players got screwed out of a dream trip to California. Imagine their angst. Duke beat Oregon State in that game, but traditionally, the Blue Devils played a quality of football that schools with an elevated scholarly ranking were supposed to play.

That changed in 2013 under coach David Cutcliff, and if the team continues to perform at that level, then Cutcliff will soon be coaching someplace good, like Florida. The Aggies were listed as twelve-point favorites for the bowl game, and omen freaks might have found that disturbing because they had been twelve-point favorites over Auburn, too. Concerns like that were actually confirmed during the first half of the Chick-fil-A Bowl.

Things were bad from the outset. Mike Evans, the great receiver, had clearly been the victim of pass interference on an early possession, but the official blew the call. Evans protested so vehemently that the Aggies were charged with the fifteen-yard penalty instead of vice versa. The Aggies' defense had finished the regular season ranked last in the SEC, and against the Blue Devils, they demonstrated why. On six first-half possessions, Duke scored five touchdowns and a field goal, and after the first half hour of playing time, the Aggies were down 38–17.

Johnny Football's Aggie finale was going up in smoke, but Johnny Football was too dynamic a personality to allow that to happen. The box score of the Chick-fil-A Bowl would note that in the third quarter, Manziel completed a nineteen-yard touchdown pass to Travis Labhart. The story behind that play, though, contained all of the elements that make up the Manziel legend. Over sixty-seven thousand people inside the Georgia Dome experienced yet another one of those "I can't believe what I think I just saw" plays that Manziel, and only Manziel, could perform. Under duress from the blitzing Duke defense, Manziel took off like a man being pursued by the Keystone Kops. The chase scene seemed to last five minutes, and at one point, Manziel collided with one of his own linemen and kept on dancing and dodging until, at the very last moment, he flung the ball to his receiver in the end zone.

Manziel and one of the zebras simultaneously extended both arms into the air to signal TD. The Aggies were on their way back, and anybody who had followed the Manziel show for the last two years realized that he would save the day. That Aggie defense, so often relegated to leper-colony status during the long season, would be redeemed. Tony Hurd ran an interception back thirty-three yards for a touchdown. Linebacker Nate Askew made a pick with 1:19 left, and the Aggies—at one point down by twenty points—won the game 52–48. It was a picture-perfect conclusion to Manziel's incomparable college career.

It was a gratifying moment. With his college eligibility finally terminated by the formality of his application as an early entry to the pro draft, Manziel could autograph souvenir merchandise until his hand bled and take all the cash he wanted. His next move was quintessentially Johnny Football. January can be cold and raw in College Station, so Manziel, along with Mike Evans, moved to San Diego, California, where the pair shared a rented house and embarked upon a full-phase self-improvement program to refine their skills in the face of the upcoming draft. Manziel, spending family dollars, retained a personal trainer, a passing tutor to help refine his grip on the ball and perfect his footwork technique, a nutrition expert, and a chef.

In the meantime, a legion of commentators from deep within the core of cluelessness that lies in the heart of the National Football League propaganda machine was cranking out the good old barnyard manure. It was fashionable to pinpoint reasons why Manziel was unfit for high draft duty. The league had forever made a living by promoting the notion that its players actually descended from Mount Olympus every Sunday to amuse themselves by entertaining the masses. Fact was, in terms of sheer athletic prowess, the NFL was dramatically inferior to the NBA and MLB and, in many cases, leading names from the ranks of the National Bowling Congress.

One writer from NFL.com deemed Manziel an "arrogant prima donna." The writer, of course, had never met Manziel. It never occurred to him that a twenty-year-old kid having a good time does not constitute arrogance and that teams don't unite and rally around a player—like the Aggies had done with Johnny Manziel—if the player is a prima donna or anything close to one.

Other complaints involved what they deemed to be Manziel's lack of height. They predicted that his running proclivities would result in frequent injuries, if not sudden death. What they failed to comprehend was that Manziel possessed a necessary component that might be described as torque: he had the innate knack for twisting his body in a fashion that enabled him to avoid the full impact of the big hit. That skill is something that cannot be taught. Many NFL quarterbacks lack it, most notably Troy Aikman, former star QB with the Cowboys. When Aikman ran with the ball, he looked about as elusive as Gort, the robot from *The Day the Earth Stood Still*. Aikman sustained so many direct hits, whether from broadside or head on, it remains a miracle that he can remember his own name.

Plenty of people, Manziel among them, pointed out Russell Wilson, quarterback of the Super Bowl champions, as an example of the shorter, more mobile quarterback who has not only survived but thrived in the NFL. Actually, a more apt example of a player with Manziel's skill set—someone whom the doubters have curiously overlooked or forgotten—is a quarterback named Fran Tarkenton from another time, another generation. He starred mostly with the Minnesota Vikings and also played for the Giants. Tarkenton was an unapologetic scrambler, played for fifteen seasons, and never missed a game due to injury.

Like Manziel, Tarkenton was six feet tall. Well, the doubters would probably contend, he played at a time when the league was less physical than the present-day version. Wrong. Tarkenton played against the likes of Dick Butkus and Joe Greene and a broad array of football personalities well-versed in the high art of decapitation.

As of this writing, Manziel is en route to the annual scouting combine in Indianapolis and will subject himself to the scrutiny of people who will count his bench-presses, time his forty-yard dash, measure his vertical jump, and of course issue him the fifty-question, multiple-choice Wonderlic cognitive skills test in which football players ponder brain-busters like, "You go into a liquor store that has five bottles of cheap wine. After you have tied up the clerk and run out of the store with three bottles, how many bottles of cheap wine are left in the store?"

All of the evaluations at the scouting combine actually have little or no real value when it comes to determining a pro football candidate's real potential, particularly the quarterbacks. What they can't measure is the one something that makes Johnny Football so rare. That is a God-given knack of anticipation, the gift of visualizing an event before it takes place, the something "that makes the good ones great." Like Joe Montana. Or Michael Jordan. Or Magic Johnson. Or Wayne Gretzky. That "something" is the reason why a couple of billboards seen in Houston demanded that the Texans use that hard-earned No. 1 draft choice on Johnny Manziel.

The future, with all of its beguiling unknowns, beckons Manziel. One thing remains certain. Some Texas Aggies might not have liked the quarterback's notorious tweet from his crazy days of 2013, but it was now time to say farewell to Johnny Football. They will never see another one like him.

ACKNOWLEDGMENTS

PEOPLE WHO WRITE BOOKS have been known to complain that their task is a lonely one. For people like Edgar Allan Poe, that might have been true. In the case of a nonfiction sports book, the most satisfying element of the project is that the writer becomes the beneficiary of gratifying interchange with an extending family of extremely enlightened and entertaining individuals.

That certainly came into play during this project, and I especially wish to forward my appreciation and thanks to the following folks:

Bo Carter, former media director for the Big 12 Conference and coauthor of the book *Tales from Aggieland*, Brad Stribling, Tom Stephenson, Whit Canning, Billy Wolfson, Cameron Young, Jim Greer of County Cork in Ireland, Jim Iman, Leon Walters, Johnny Langdon and the Bumbershoot Productions people, Chance Steed of Fort Worth (the twenty-three-thousand-square-foot Netum A. Steed Physiology and Conditioning Laboratory that serves as the weight room for all Texas Aggie athletes is named in honor of this grandfather), and Coach Eddie Shirley, now of Lubbock, Texas.

Research sources were numerous, but the sports website *Deadspin* offered a valuable resource with its story concerning Johnny Manziel's family tree. That report contained more great information than probably the rest of the national media stories concerning the saga of Johnny Football combined. Warren St. John's book *Rammer Jammer Yellow Hammer* offered great insight into the depth of football fan mania in the Deep South. As always, the downtown Dallas Public Library served as one of my favorite haunts. In that regard, I'd also like to commend the Half-Price Books store on Preston Road in North Dallas for also selling a really good pair of half-price glasses that enabled me to read the grainy microfilm on those machines at the library.

Many thanks to Jeff Serena and all of the rest of his editorial and production team at MVP Books, and also to my longtime literary rep, Joe Vallely, CEO of Swagger Press.

On the home front, everlasting gratitude goes to my wife, Karen G. Shropshire, and my son, P.C., who was skillful at locating various imperfections that appeared in the first draft of the manuscript.

Gig 'em!

—Mike Shropshire, Dallas, 2014

INDEX